Free Markets Under Siege

HOOVER CLASSICS

The Hoover Classics series will reissue selected books of lasting merit and influence from the list of previous Hoover Institution Press publications. The aim of the series is to engender new interest in these titles and expand the readership to a wider audience—in some cases, to a new generation. Additionally, it is hoped that by extending the life of these books, they will continue to contribute to free discussion and debate on important issues of public policy and historical understanding.

Robert E. Hall and Alvin Rabushka,
The Flat Tax, second edition

Richard Epstein,
*Free Markets Under Siege:
Cartels, Politics, and Social Welfare*

Russell A. Berman,
*Anti-Americanism in Europe:
A Cultural Problem*

Free Markets Under Siege

Cartels, Politics, and Social Welfare

by
Richard A. Epstein

with a Foreword by
Sir Geoffrey Owen

and Commentary by
Geoffrey Wood

Hoover Institution Press
Stanford University
Stanford, California

www.hoover.org

Hoover Institution Press Publication No. 536

First American paperback edition published in 2005

First printing Hoover Classics edition, 2008
14   13   12   11   10   09   08   9   8   7   6   5   4   3   2   1

Manufactured in the United States of America

The paper used in this publication meets the minimum requirements
of American National Standard for Information Sciences—Permanence
of Paper for Printed Library Materials, ANSI Z39.48-1992. ∞

Library of Congress Cataloging-in-Publication Data

Epstein, Richard Allen, 1943–
Free markets under siege : cartels, politics, & social welfare /
by Richard A. Epstein ; with a foreword by Sir Geoffrey Owen
and commentary by Geoffrey Wood.
        p.   cm. — (Hoover classics)
(Hoover Institution press publication ; no. 536)
"Reissued with a new introduction."
Includes bibliographical references and index.
ISBN-13: 978-0-8179-4611-1 (cloth: alk. paper)
  1. Capitalism. 2. Socialism. 3. Competition.
I. Wood, Geoffrey, 1925–   II. Title.
HB501.E648 2008
330.12′2—dc22   2007034033

Contents

Introduction to the Hoover Classics Edition   vii

Foreword by Sir Geoffrey Owen   xix

Brief Introduction to the American Edition:
Back Home Again   xxiii

1. Modern Justifications for Classical Liberalism   1

2. Between Socialism and Libertarianism   9

3. Competition and Cartels   25

4. Agricultural Markets, Protectionism,
and Cartels   33

5. Cartels in Labor Markets   51

6. Conclusion: The Importance of
Getting the Easy Cases Right   71

References   73

Commentary by Geoffrey Wood   77

Index   93

Introduction to the Hoover Classics Edition
by Richard A. Epstein

MY SHORT ESSAY, *Free Markets under Siege: Cartels, Politics, and Social Welfare*, had its origin in the Thirty-third Wincott Lecture that I delivered in London on October 13, 2003. The original English version was published by the Institute of Economic Affairs in early 2004. The volume was republished jointly later that year under the same title for Australia and New Zealand by the New Zealand Business Roundtable and Institute for Public Affairs. The first Hoover edition of the volume appeared in 2005, with an introduction for American readers. I am happy to report that a Spanish translation of the volume has been completed and will be shortly published by the Peruvian University of Applied Sciences.

The importance of this topic, I think, deserves all the attention that I and anyone else can lavish on it. The book is divided into two parts. The first half argues that the central distinction for the organization of government and political life is that between competition and protectionism. Competition produces systematic gains unrivaled by any other system of production and distribution. Protectionism relies on the use of state coercion to introduce measures that lead not only to a loss of political liberty but also to state monopolies, high tariffs, and economic stagnation. Building on these insights, the second half looks at agricultural and labor markets to show the baleful results that ensue when political forces displace economic competition with an unwholesome mixture of subsidies and barriers to entry. In this introduction, I shall not review anew the arguments that lead inexorably to this conclusion. Rather my purpose in the summer of 2007 is to comment on the state of the long-standing struggle between competition and protectionism in the nearly four years since the London lecture.

The scorecard on that contest is at best mixed. I have little doubt that in those areas where the competitive, or free market, program, has been put into play its benefits are immediate. One component of the overall system is low and flat taxes, and without question the Bush tax reforms have been a great success in the United States. Furthermore, the stunning Estonian reforms of the past decade offer an even more powerful confirmation of the wisdom of the system. Lower taxes increase the returns of both capital and labor, allowing government revenues to expand with the increased size of the pie. The net effect is that government revenues increase when it takes a smaller share of the larger social pie. More important, that program leaves greater amounts of wealth in private hands, where it can be more efficiently directed toward investment or consumption as people see fit.

I would like to think that the congruence between the basic principle and the observed outcome would lead people on all sides of the political spectrum to spurn the repeated calls for higher taxation. Nonetheless these calls continue unabated. The case rests on the quaint assumption that the rich don't really "need" their money so that the one-two punch of progressive taxation and a stiff increase in capital gains rates offer painless ways to fund domestic programs. It is discouraging to hear prominent politicians speak as if redistribution were a costless goal best achieved through increased state coercion, which in practice will only bring in its wake some unhappy combination of renewed efforts at tax evasion and reduced levels of output. The only assumption in this debate that is sure to be wrong is that changes in the structure of taxation defended on distributional grounds will otherwise exert no influence on output, prices, or production. The truth is, if anything, close to the opposite: changes in the tax structure will influence, for better or worse, the conduct of virtually all individuals in a thousand ways, none of which corresponds to the naïve view that a massive change in wealth distribution offers low-hanging fruit for any government with the courage to pick it.

The stark conflict between economic theory and political rhetoric has troubling implications. To my mind, the key challenge of public affairs is not to develop economic models that offer evermore sophisticated analyses of complex forms of individual behavior under conditions of uncertainty. Rather, it is to make it clear to the public at large that its deep bias in favor of high taxes and, for that matter, increased regulation rests on fundamental misconceptions. This is no small order. Professor Bryan Caplan has published a sobering volume, *The Myth of the Rational Voter: Why Democracies Choose Bad Policies* (Princeton University Press 2007), which advances the thesis that democratic institutions have a strong bias to move in the wrong direction on economic matters because of the *systematic* ignorance of the public at large. That view comes into sharp conflict with the usual conclusions of public choice theory insofar as it discredits the assumption that all individuals act in a rational, relentless, and self-interested fashion in the political arena just as they do in their private contexts.

It turns out that any theory of public choice is incomplete and inaccurate insofar as it assumes that all the people fully understand the implications of their positions on matters of great political concern. This makes the problem of government still more difficult because we must add the problem of ignorance to the problem of faction, without knowing how these two pervasive forces interact in a wide range of political settings. Neither should we be surprised about the difficulties of public deliberation on these critical matters of economic organization. First, there is a perfectly rational explanation for people handling their private affairs better than they do voting or deliberating on the large issues of the day. The learning mechanism for understanding the often adverse consequences of personal decisions does not rest on the cognitive ability to understand the interrelationship between supply and demand or the economic proposition that all decisions are made at the margin. Rather, the feedback mechanisms that lead people to make corrections, however haltingly, in their daily lives are that they *personally* suffer the consequences of spending too much or buying the wrong goods and services.

In making their public choices, however, these same people, now voters, have no such direct feedback mechanism. Worse still, our dizzying world offers few natural experiments whose outcomes are easy to observe. On the contrary, the constant barrage of stimuli means that the *indirect* consequences of various government programs are ignored and that the direct consequences of those programs are given far too much weight. In the area of taxation, for example, the direct consequence of higher taxes is that richer people pay a larger fraction of their income and poorer people pay fewer taxes or none at all. Thus, measured by its intended consequences, a program of higher taxes looks as though it will have its desired effects. Only by studying the theory can people learn that those changes will usher in a myriad of private decisions dealing with investment, hiring, consumption, and the like. One great advantage of the flat tax, for instance, is that it minimizes the incentives for strategic behavior and the chances of error in calculation: no one need create cumbersome devices for income splitting when marginal tax rates equal average rates. But those benefits of simplicity in taxes, or regulation, can be gotten across only through education, which is hard to transmit over the political din.

The situation is still more complex because the distribution of ignorance is not random. Those interest groups at the heart of the fray—no matter what their stripe or cause—are often well aware of the long-term consequences of their initiatives. Yet once such groups gain influence, their agenda—whether in the form of punitive taxes on rivals or special tax breaks for themselves—is to steer wealth, opportunity, and power in their direction and away from competitors. If those groups can form alliances with independent, civic-minded groups and thus hide their self-interest, these potent coalitions of strange bedfellows can easily carry the day in democratic politics.

In this regard, because of the total lack of any clear message on these critical economic issues by any political leader of national stature, today's domestic outlook is somewhat pessimistic. Now, close to twenty years from the time Ronald Reagan left office, in January 1989, we can clearly identify, as Martin and Annelise Anderson have documented in *Reagan in His Own Hand*, the great, if sometimes unsung, edge that defined the Reagan presidency: he learned and internalized the important lessons of classical liberalism, with its emphasis on limited government, low taxes, strong markets, and self-reliance. Reagan was a great communicator because he had something to say. Neither of his two (Bush) successors have been able to articulate, or indeed accept, his program with sufficient clarity and conviction to offset the big-government rhetoric that dominates and corrodes public deliberation and debate.

The consequences of this breakdown in public discourse are not confined to matters of taxation. They seep into just about every domestic and foreign policy issue. In July 2007, the federal minimum wage rose from

$5.15. to $5.85 (with additional $0.70 increases in July 2008 and July 2009), an initiative that met with intellectual resistance from economically minded individuals but faced no true political opposition in Congress on either side of the aisle. The usual platitudes carried the day: the minimum wage would raise the wages of those at the bottom, without creating dislocations elsewhere. The second part of that statement would be true if the statutory minimum were set below the market wage. But the two parts of the sentence cannot be true together because employers will take steps to minimize their costs, thereby creating some short-time dislocations and hurting the long-term prospects of the poorest and least-educated individuals, those with, at best, a toehold in the market.

The same sort of political rhetoric has, fortunately, taken less of a toll in the recent debates over the rise in gasoline prices. Even though too many people still think that some hidden form of greed or monopolization is at work, many realize that what is actually happening are sensible and continuous adjustments in prices to reflect shifts in supply and demand, in both directions. Thus the populists condemn the rise (but never the fall) in the price of standard commodities and often seek to punish the very actions that help ration goods with increased scarcity value. I suspect that the demands for maximum price controls on gasoline, although commonly voiced, have not been as successful as the calls to hike the minimum wage because enough people remember the long queues that formed when Richard Nixon imposed price controls on gasoline in the early

1970s. It turned out that we were not immune to government-induced shortages that replicated the endless lines characteristic of the Soviet system.

The consequences of political mistakes are not confined to domestic issues but also exert a vast influence on foreign relations. Some sense of the depth of ignorance on this issue was captured by then presidential candidate John Kerry, who spoke of CEOs who sought to outsource work from the United States to foreign countries as Benedict Arnolds, a sentiment which was echoed by his Republican rival, George W. Bush. Such remarks are far off base: Benedict Arnold was a traitor who plotted to turn over West Point to the British during the Revolutionary War. Should we really equate CEOs who seek to lower costs and improve quality with people disloyal to the United States? That position garners public respectability for one familiar reason: it studiously avoids the indirect benefits of these sensible maneuvers in a world economy, both here and abroad.

Domestic American protectionist sentiments hurt our credibility overseas, which I hope to exemplify with a personal anecdote. I still remember my acute embarrassment when, in the spring of 2003, I was asked to defend open markets before an economic meeting in Brussels, the headquarters of the European Union, shortly after President Bush had announced that he was putting tariffs on imported steel to shore up his political position in Pennsylvania or West Virginia. Fortunately, the tariffs were eventually removed, but not without protest. It took some twenty months to contain but not eliminate the dangers. Lifting is better than keeping, but it is far from ideal, especially when said removal is not accompanied by a candid recognition of the initial error and a solemn vow never to repeat it. Instead we declared victory, announcing that the tariffs had achieved their goal because the steel industry had "wisely" used the time for consolidation and restructuring, which could have been done more efficiently if the temporary protection had never been supplied.

Unfortunately, that episode has not proved to be an isolated incident, given the increased willingness on all sides to use transient expedients to justify other restraints on international trade. All too often tariff walls in the United States erect barriers to goods from countries whose political support we desperately need. The situation is no better on the question of subsidies, for lavish farm subsidies distort the domestic market and create (this time for real) unfair competition against the produce of poorer nations who cannot compete with subsidized American goods in world markets. The beat does not end there. As this introduction was being written, relationships between the United States and Peru were strained because of U.S. insistence that Peru enact certain domestic reforms in labor and environmental matters as a condition of a free trade agreement with the United States. The folly of this approach lies not in the particulars of the terms that are demanded but in linking free trade to domestic reform in other countries. Free trade is itself a great reformer: the input of cheap goods and services from foreign sources acts as a powerful and persistent spur to domestic reform that no local firm or union can evade as long as the tariff barriers remain low.

The most notable illustration of this proposition is the enormous expansion in output and profitability of New Zealand agriculture after its inordinate subsidies were removed at one stroke in the mid 1980s. Make no mistake, the true purpose of such proposed U.S. restrictions is to make exports from those countries more expensive, meaning that protectionists at home get an imperfect substitute for the tariff barriers that are about to be lowered. How ironic it is that the price for free trade in foreign countries is the acceptance of external controls on labor and other markets that those countries do not seek to impose on themselves.

The same situation can be observed in the constant struggle over immigration into the United States. The first, and most tragic, point is that one consequence of our strong welfare state is that it makes more respectable demands for limiting immigration into the United States: How, such arguments go, do we know whether people from overseas are coming to this country to work or to receive a generous package of welfare benefits paid for by others? That problem would not arise were those benefits smaller. But now that they are fixed in the domestic political market, a heavy price is paid by foreigners who are shut out of this country in larger numbers than is appropriate.

Yet the protectionist elements have proved powerful in the recent immigration debate, especially with the shortage of coveted H-1B visas for highly skilled workers who are needed to power our high-tech efforts in biotechnology and computers, as once again a bipartisan coalition seeks to block or reduce entry. Those limited visas are snapped up the day the government makes them available. Efforts are now under way to require such skilled workers to receive the prevailing American wage, as a clear barrier against entry. But any effort to expand the pool of eligible entrants is met with fierce protectionist resistance from people who see new immigrants only as competitors for American workers, not as current or future suppliers, colleagues, buyers, or prospective founders of businesses and employers of thousands. Once again that narrow perspective, which sees only harm from direct competition, has taken over the public debate.

To these intellectual follies, the only answer is education. As Caplan's research indicates, the public at large takes the wrong position on just about every issue relating to domestic issues of business and labor, international issues, and tariffs, trade, and immigration. The educated public, however, does far better on these issues than the public at large, to whom politicians of both parties pander. The most important economic and social issues of our time depend on lifting the siege that today surrounds the operation of free markets. I am proud and pleased that the Hoover Institution, true to its basic mission, has seen fit to reissue this volume under its Hoover Classics imprint, especially so soon after its original publication. I hope it will embolden the proponents of free trade, both at home and abroad.

Foreword

ONE OF THE AIMS of the Wincott Foundation is to contribute to a better understanding of how markets work and to highlight the damage that can be caused to social welfare when market forces are suppressed to serve the narrow aims of special interest groups. These themes figured prominently in the writings of Harold Wincott, the financial journalist in whose honor the foundation was set up in 1960, and they have been articulated in several of the Wincott lectures, which have been held annually since that date.

The 2003 Wincott lecture, delivered by Professor Richard Epstein from the University of Chicago and published in extended form in this paper, provided an illuminating analysis of some of the ways in which interest groups, aided and abetted by sympathetic politicians, have been able to rig the market in their favor. Professor Epstein focused in particular on two areas where such intervention has been extensive and persistent in the United States and western Europe — agriculture and the labor market.

On the first, Professor Epstein showed how the "right to farm," proclaimed by President Franklin Roosevelt in his 1944 State of the Union address, was transformed into the right of an individual to remain indefinitely in a particular occupation, whatever changes in supply and demand might take place. This arrangement was bolstered by an elaborate array of subsidies and restrictions designed to preserve the status quo, at considerable cost to taxpayers and consumers. Although the damage has been offset, at least in the advanced industrial countries, by spectacular improvements in agricultural productivity, Professor Epstein pointed out that the gains from technology are not spread evenly around the world and that agricultural protection imposes great damage on developing countries, which are prevented from making full use of their advantages of climate and cheap labor.

As for the labor market, the lecture contained a fascinating account of how procompetitive rulings by the U.S. Supreme Court in 1908 and 1917 were subsequently undermined by political decisions to exempt trade unions from the scope of the antitrust laws and then to regulate collective bargaining through the National Labor Relations Act. The consequence was the statutory codification of monopoly over competition. Fortunately, the effect of these measures was somewhat blunted by the Taft-Hartley Act of 1947, which restricted the ability of unions to bring pressure on employers through secondary boycotts and in other ways. Even more important was the impact of foreign competition: the postwar change in public attitudes toward free trade has had a strong market-positive influence on the degree of trade union power.

Professor Epstein related these cases to the larger issue of how best to regulate the interface between market choice and government behavior. Drawing on his deep knowledge of history, law, and economics, he discussed the need to find a middle way between socialism and libertarianism. The libertarians, he suggested, have gotten many things right, not least in their stress on the social gains that arise from voluntary exchange, but they sometimes underplay the importance of the social infrastructure—including a system of public taxation and finance—which no market can supply.

The great challenge for liberal democracies is to work out how to use systems of coercion to benefit the individuals and institutions subjected to it. In Epstein's view, it is possible to devise rules that permit the provision of public goods without allowing the state to succumb to the political favoritism that leads to massive transfers of wealth from one faction to another.

Professor Epstein presented his arguments with clarity, force, and wit—qualities that were very much in evidence during the lively discussion following his lecture. The trustees of the Wincott Foundation are grateful to Professor Epstein for agreeing to deliver the lecture, and warmly commend this paper.

Sir Geoffrey Owen
Chairman of the Trustees
The Wincott Foundation

Brief Introduction to the American Edition: Back Home Again

IN OCTOBER 2003, I had the great honor to deliver the Wincott lecture in London. The lecture was entitled *Free Markets Under Siege*, and after it was given, an expanded version of the essay was published, along with a commentary by Professor Geoffrey Wood of the Cass Business School. The essay deals with some broad issues on the interaction of markets and regulation in the United States and England. As is evident from the table of contents, this essay is divided into theoretical and applied halves. The first portion, which deals with the larger questions of political organization, has as its central theme that the ultimate contest between classical liberal and socialist ideals depends on the ability of each to solve the large questions surrounding the production and distribution of goods. On that question, I argue that there is little doubt that the classical liberal solution, with its stress on limited government, strong property rights, and free exchange, will outperform any command-and-control economy. That judgment depends on how these rival systems respond to basic problems of production and exchange, even if we cannot be confident of the best response to some of the hardest issues of this or any other area—for example, what is the proper mode for the location of large public facilities, and how should they be financed? If we get the big questions right, then we can survive the errors that we make on the remaining, difficult second-order questions.

The themes in question travel well. This essay has already been reproduced for the Australian and New Zealand markets. I am happy that it will now be published by the Hoover Institution for circulation in the American market. The publication of this volume at home makes perfect sense, because the book explores, in broad outline, the historical interplay between American constitutional doctrine and American economic development. It would be nice to report that our constitutional founders reached the right decision on every key point related to social and economic development, so that everything thereafter could be regarded as a fall from grace. But it is quite clear that they did not, for all great ventures contain their own fair share of mistakes. For example, the founders showed too great a willingness to allow the nation to be surrounded by a strong set of tariff walls. Although their efforts were far from perfect, however, they grasped, in large measure, the central truth about political organization. In general, they showed a lively appreciation for the risk of factions and, thus, sought to organize their political institutions in ways that would minimize these risks by dividing authority between state and national government and by separating the powers of the national government into three distinct branches, which made possible the use of checks and balances among them. The founders had a strong appreciation that a successful nation requires strong government that is focused in its operation of providing peace and security on the one hand and an adequate social infrastructure on the other. They were cognizant that the risk of too much government had to be balanced against the risk of too little.

Yet over time, many of these insights were lost. The rise of the New Deal was spurred by the dominant beliefs of the Progressive Era that strong government responses were required in order to overcome the excessive individualism, as it was termed, of an earlier age. Writers as notable as Louis Brandeis took deep exception to the proposition that the conceptions of liberty and property that had animated Adam Smith could work in the age of industrialization with its rapid technological progress. Early convictions that the role of the state was to preserve the notion of equal liberty of all under law were dismissed as formal conceptions that did not respond to the massive inequalities of wealth and economic power in the modern age. Instead, government had to serve as a conscious counterweight to large industrial interests. The Progressives were rightly suspicious of monopoly power, but they wrongly extended their suspicious attitude of the outcome of competitive processes, which they saw not as mutually beneficial but as exploitative of ordinary workers and small businessmen.

These high-minded concerns, I believe, led the Progressives sorely astray in their articulation of economic policy and constitutional law. The only device that they could come up with to deal with the economic realities of the New Age was the creation of state-protected monopolies, frequently in agricultural and labor markets. To implement this misguided economic vision, they had to dismantle the constitutional structures that stood in their path. The earlier limitations on federal power had to be pushed aside. "Commerce among the several states" had to be read so broadly as to cover manufacturing and agriculture within each and every state; otherwise, industry and labor cartels could not be maintained. The extensive system of regulation also required limitations on the rights of private property and free contract, and these two went into eclipse under the influence of the Progressive movement. The original vision of the Constitution gave way under the pressure of an intellectual attack that was mounted both in the United States and in Great Britain. The changes in political philosophy led to a misguided transformation in constitutional worldview that offered few restraints on federal power and virtually no protections for economic liberties.

One purpose of this short volume is to trace the switch in worldview in both countries and to dispute its wisdom. The strength and innovation of competitive markets is a durable phenomenon that works as well in the twenty-first century as it did in the eighteenth. In this volume, I hope to expose the danger and folly of the deviation from those sound classical liberal principles that has led to these major constitutional and policy mistakes in the United States, as well as to parallel adjustments in the political practices in Great Britain. These issues that were once fought over are being refought on a nearly daily basis. I hope that this volume will make some small contribution toward restoring the proper constitutional and economic balance both here and abroad.

Free Markets Under Siege
Cartels, Politics,and Social Welfare

Illustration © David Bromley/*Financial Times*

1. Modern Justifications for Classical Liberalism

IT WAS A VERY GREAT HONOR to be invited to give the Wincott lecture for 2003, for it allowed me to renew a set of connections that I have long had with England. I started my legal education in Oxford in 1964, receiving a bachelor's degree in jurisprudence in 1966, after which I returned to the United States to complete my legal education at Yale in 1968. Immediately upon graduation from Yale, I took up the study and teaching of law, which became my life's work.

The combination of English and American education has proved a great advantage to me because it familiarized me with *three* legal systems: English and American are the obvious two; the Roman law system, which was then required study at Oxford, is the third. The English educational experience was essential to my intellectual development, but not perhaps as my instructors intended, for they nourished my affection for the laissez-faire tradition more by happenstance than by conscious design. The major questions in English law, then as now, were often resolved by administrative order within the vaunted civil service, which translated into the (then) regnant rule of English administrative law that all decisions of the minister should be final. The effect, therefore, was that in our curriculum, we concentrated on those matters that did not fall into the purview of minister's discretion in the administrative state. In effect, the legal education in England placed its emphasis on private law as it governed the unregulated portion of the economy. That project, in turn, required us to read a large number of nineteenth-century and earlier decisions written by judges who were congenial to voluntary contract and private property. At the same time, my study of Roman law persuaded me that the basic principles of English common law could also take hold in political settings widely different from those in modern times.

Unlike political theorists who work at an abstract level, these judges had the huge advantage of testing their basic theories against the concrete cases that cried out for decision. By the same token, these same judges often suffered from a professional disadvantage because, with a few notable exceptions, they did not ground their views in general political theory. Indeed, it is on that score that the English legal education has lagged somewhat, both then and now, for it does not place enough emphasis on the importance of interdisciplinary studies, which have been the centerpiece of American legal education for several decades at least. But an English and American legal education proved, in my case, to be happily complementary.

Having learned from two cultures, I regard my comparative advantage in this intellectual debate over the uses and limits of state power to be my ability to work as an arbitrageur between the two worlds—for, in time, I came to believe that the rules of decision in these private disputes had real relevance to the larger questions that had, in practice, been taken over by the modern administrative state. The conclusions, moreover, seemed to hold with equal force in the United States, notwithstanding the two very great differences between our legal systems: the U.S. written constitution and federalism are linked features that are, as yet, nowhere found in England. I hope that, armed with the tools of economics and political theory, I can produce theoretical arguments that explain the social desirability of certain institutions better than the ancient appeal to "natural reason." That term, which has its origin in the Roman texts, worked well enough in ages past when intuition was the dominant guide to the formation of legal policy. It counted as the leading intellectual motif for such great political and legal writers as Grotius, Locke, Pufendorf, and Blackstone, who have exerted such an enormous positive influence in modern times. But now that we have developed a stronger apparatus of economic and political theory, that form of theoretical quiescence can no longer carry the day. There is so much to say about social institutions and laws that it becomes foolhardy to regard self-evidence as the ultimate criterion of a sound legal rule, political institution, or social practice. We have to use the most modern logic and theory available—whether we want to or not—for our adversaries, whoever they may be, will rightly do the same on the other side. Fortunately, the use of the new techniques usually proves benevolent in that it helps us justify, in a modern idiom, the results of these earlier writers in terms more robust than they could supply for their own deeply held intuitions. Our job, therefore, is neither to junk their conclusions nor to belittle their efforts. It is to engage in an intelligent reconstruction of great ideas that have withstood the test of time.

My more immediate connection to England relates directly to Harold Wincott and the *Financial Times*. It leads to one of the central themes of this lecture. The *Financial Times* was kind enough to publish an article of mine in its October 13, 2003, edition. It began with a picture (reproduced as the frontispiece to this chapter) that relates to the topic of this talk—first gather the low-hanging fruit—but that, I fear, not even the most astute reader could decipher. The picture shows a tree with a lot of apples. On one side, there are people standing on the ground, reaching out and grabbing the apples; on the other side stand people with ladders and hoists trying to figure out how they can climb up to gather the apples at the top of the tree. The obvious query is: what on earth does a picture of a tree with a collection of apples have to do with the question of how to organize different markets? As I looked at the illustration, I would have said that the picture contained an oblique reference to the temptation and fall of Adam and Eve as evidence that the private appropriation of natural resources is the source of all evil in the world. But my column had no such devious intention. To clarify matters, therefore, I will take a moment to explain what the picture is about because, in fact, it highlights the central theme of this lecture: first and foremost, get the easy cases right, and then worry about the hard cases later.

Here is how I reached this conclusion. The study of any complex social system leads, on reflection, to the comforting observation that the world contains easy and hard cases. The following characteristics are true of hard cases: they require a huge expenditure of intellectual energy in order to figure out their solution, and yet, measured against some social ideal, our best choices invariably suffer from a very high rate of error, even when we do our level best. The happy side of this process is that we are likely to be damned no matter which alternative we embrace. So, if the law seeks to determine a very complicated issue, such as the optimum duration of a patent, it is easy to identify an infinite set of permutations, because the question of patent duration cannot be effectively decided in isolation without reference to patent scope, itself a highly technical area. To make matters worse, the field of patentable inventions might be too broad for a general solution to the problem. For example, the answer that seems to work well for pharmaceutical patents may not be as sensible for software patents. But the moment we decide that different patent classes should have different durations, then someone will be faced with the unhappy task of classifying a new generation of inventions that regrettably straddles a pre-existing set of categories established in ignorance of the future path of technical development. Such is the case with computer software, for example. Given this shifting background, it is very difficult to conclude authoritatively that one patent duration rather than another is the best. Of course, we can make credible arguments that patent duration should be far shorter than copyright duration, but that does not fix an appropriate length of time for either form of intellectual property. In the end, the best answers rely on educated hunches by persons who work within the field, who may differ substantially in their conclusions.

In some cases, the problems get even more difficult than patent duration because of the discontinuous nature of the basic choice. All too often, the world does not allow us the luxury of continually fine-tuning responses until we approach some social ideal. The question of whether to build a new airport or highway or rail system gives rise to an initial "yes or no" choice. Once that basic commitment is made, it will, of course, be followed by a host of smaller decisions, some of which can be fine-tuned, but others, not. The advantages and disadvantages of the basic choice are hard to foresee and are equally hard to evaluate quantitatively even when foreseen. Just think of how hard it is to estimate the impact of a new airport on noise, pollution, traffic, land values, business growth, and the like. The only thing we can say with certainty is that some affected persons will win and others will lose. Yet it is no mean feat to examine which persons fall into which class or to determine how much compensation, if any, is owing to those persons who are inconvenienced by the process. The difficulty of the subject matter and the nature of the political process restrict us to sharply discontinuous solutions, all of which could be far removed from the social ideal. Any choice is likely to contain large errors; but the same is not necessarily true of the *difference* in errors between two solutions. That figure could be small. Thus, if one error goes high by 1000, and the other, low by 1000, then the error levels could be enormous, but equally balanced. In this midst of our travail, we ought to take comfort in the thought that so long as people do their level best to get the hard cases right, then we should not protest too loudly if they get them wrong. The chances are that other people would have made similar mistakes, and we will never get able people to work on difficult social projects as long as we insist on judging their handiwork harshly with the benefit of hindsight. Our standard of criticism has to respect the decisions made in good faith by persons in positions of responsibility, so that they are not hauled into the dock when it appears they made the wrong decision. This prinicple lies at the core of the doctrine of official immunity. We have to learn to both live and prosper in a second-best world.

The appropriate response to hard cases, then, is an uneasy mix between patience and deference. The easy cases, in contrast, turn out to be miraculously important for the day-to-day operations of any system precisely because we can be confident that the wrong decision will lead to serious social dislocations with few offsetting benefits. This proposition holds for how a society draws the interface between market choice and government behavior, which is my main theme. But once again, we have to keep the basic point about economic organization in perspective. The truly great social catastrophes do not come from a misapplication of the basic principles of a market economy. They arise from a wholesale disrespect for individual liberty, which is manifested in tolerated lynchings and arbitrary arrests, and from a total contempt for private property, through its outright seizure by government forces intent on stifling opposition or lining their own pockets. The reason Great Britain and the United States did not go the way of Germany and the Soviet Union in the turmoil of the 1930s was that the political institutions in both countries were able to hold firm against these palpable excesses, even as they went astray on a host of smaller economic issues.

It was the failure to grasp this point clearly that led Friedrich Hayek, in *The Road to Serfdom* (1944), to be too gloomy about the fate of democratic institutions in western Europe and the United States. Socialism does not always lead to national socialism, so long as these critical minimum conditions for political freedom are respected across the political spectrum. Once this distinction is kept in mind, it becomes clear why we can properly count Franklin D. Roosevelt as a great American president on the political frontier even while taking strong exception, as I shall do, to the misguided economic policies that permeated his New Deal. Roosevelt's contemporary competition in the category of world historical figures was Adolf Hitler, Joseph Stalin, Mao Tse-tung, and Chiang Kai-shek. In that group, Roosevelt, along with Winston Churchill, stood tall as a beacon of liberty in a world that had plunged into disaster. Conrad Black (2003) may well be right to hail Roosevelt as a great figure, and even as the saviour of capitalism, but Roosevelt's success on the political level should not blind us to his shortfalls on the matters of economic and legal policy, especially on the matters of agriculture and labor, which are the central theme of this lecture.

2. Between Socialism and Libertarianism

ON THE QUESTION of what is the proper form for organizing the means of production, to use the Marxist
phrase, there is a wide range of disagreement over
whether a system of voluntary, competitive markets will
supply the best mix of goods and services to the popu-
lation at large. Even if we remember not to elevate this
issue to a matter of life and death, by the same token,
we should not veer too far in the opposite direction by
lapsing into a form of economic fatalism, which holds
that society's social ills will remain at some constant
level no matter what kind of economic system we adopt.
On the contrary, the level of social prosperity, and with
it political peace, depends heavily on the answers that
we collectively give to these economic and legal issues.
Getting the issues right in the easy cases should not be
greeted with stony indifference, even in comparison
with the larger political issues we face.

EASY CASES AND DIFFICULT CASES

In delineating the proper role for the market and the
state, it is vital for people who believe in the principles
of liberal democracy, as I do and as Harold Wincott did,
to get the easy cases right, even if they cannot reach
firm agreement on the difficult questions, such as patent

scope and airport location. In this spirit, I shall now concentrate on the easy cases and put the harder cases to one side. I hope to show how, far from reaching the appropriate classical liberal solutions to these problems, our political institutions frequently (but thankfully not universally) do everything backward, often in the worst possible manner. Institutional arrangements that should be a dull subject, not worthy of any discourse or conversation, become the object of intensive study in economic pathology to explain how societies first make one wrong step, only to follow that mistake with others, setting in motion a downward cycle that creates unnecessary social losses all along the way.

To frame this part of the argument, I think it is important to articulate the proper baseline for analysis. In my new book, *Skepticism and Freedom* (Epstein, 2003), I defend, as I have done for many years, a vision of classical liberalism that avoids two kinds of perils. One is the peril associated with an unyielding devotion to an unvarnished and incautious libertarian philosophy. The other is the greater peril that comes from embracing socialism or collectivism in all its forms. The issue is how to find the middle way between these two extremes.

I should not need to dwell at length on the weaknesses of collectivism as a system for controlling the means of production. It should suffice to note that no individual has either the knowledge or the selflessness to make vital decisions for other individuals. The high aspirations of collective ownership are always dashed by the grubby particulars of its practical realization. But this simple point has not always carried the day, so a few more words are needed on the topic. In particular, it is instructive to recall the powerful claims that were voiced on collectivism's behalf during the socialist calculation debate of the 1930s and 1940s. The basic claim was that a large computer could generate all the information about what goods and services should be produced under what conditions. Markets were not thought of as generative institutions, so the hope was that state planners could rig the rules of the game to approximate the ideal mix of goods and services that markets are (supposed) to generate. This could then be happily married to an income policy that narrowed the gap between rich and poor.

It is a tribute to the work of Friedrich Hayek that no one today quite believes this fantasy could be brought to successful completion, even though computers are a billion times more efficient now than they were when the socialist calculation debate took place. This utopian proposal is doomed to failure because all interested parties in the planning debacle, both public and private, will have equal access to these devices, no matter how powerful. As the night follows the day, every clever government intervention will invite multiple private responses, which are certain to undo whatever good might have come about if dedicated government officials (itself a generous assumption) had exclusive use of the new technologies involved. The hope that we could keep the distribution, be it of income or wealth, on one axis and the production of goods and services on a second axis, such that the twain will never meet, has disappeared into the dustbin of history. The single strongest safeguard that we have against excessive planning stems from the awareness that even its champions have that any government initiative, however noble, marks only the first step in what promises to be a long and arduous multiple-period game—a game in which it is hard to say with confidence that any one player could emerge victorious. Caution with respect to means may well slow down individuals and groups that maintain strong collective ideals about the choice of ends—most notably, the compression of income differentials through social planning.

The argument today, therefore, has switched grounds. No longer is it said that the state can outperform the market. Rather it is said that the market itself suffers from certain "failures" that justify forms of state intervention to protect individuals who are hurt in the process. The movement toward collectivization of all public activities, if it is to take place today, will not rest on a single bold initiative that casts aside the private sector. Instead, it will take place in the form of a multiple attack along different margins, where each individual struggle does not generalize easily across the board. The long-standing objective of the modern closet socialist is to consolidate the separate beachheads after they are taken over. Thus, state dominance can be portrayed as a device that takes the irrationality, impersonality, and cruelty out of markets and not as a device that dispenses with their use altogether. In effect, the discourse takes the form of an intellectual two-step. Step one: markets are all right when they work. Step two: but markets do not work in this particular area, be it health care, labor, housing, agriculture, or whatever, each with its own "special" problems. In one sense, the quiet blessing in this approach is that it obviates the risk of a catastrophic conversion to state control through aggressive nationalization. But it gives rise to a multiple-front war in which substantial chunks of voluntary markets always find themselves at risk. The case against overall socialism is irrefutable today. But the desire to keep up with its egalitarian objectives continues to exert a considerable influence in practice. There is little reason to think that the intellectual foundations of the collective impulse are strong enough to serve as the foundation for a more viable and comprehensive philosophy. However, we still have to keep in mind the importance that market failures have in the overall analysis when it comes to the examination of the libertarian alternative.

STRENGTHS AND WEAKNESSES OF LIBERTARIAN THOUGHT

Even if socialism may be dispatched in a few sentences, it is far more profitable to devote some words to the commendable strengths and serious drawbacks of libertarian thought. I will start with the positives and then move on to the limitations. Without question, the sensible libertarian understands the importance of property rights, of voluntary exchange, and of keeping to a minimum state devices that could upset the precarious balance created by strong property institutions. The presumption against the use of state power means that

libertarians are rightly sensitive to the problems associated with the use of force on the one hand and the
various kinds of deceptions that individuals can play
upon each other on the other. The good libertarian does
not fall into the socialist trap of thinking that any individuals can rise above human failings only when they
are placed in a position of high power, where the temp-
tations are likely to intensify. Rather, the good libertarian starts with a reasonably astute estimation of human
character. The libertarian is not somebody who believes
we are all dewy-eyed individuals who will always work
for the best interests of other people. Rather, he recognizes that self-interest is a force that is sometimes turned
into bad ends and sometimes into good ends. Armed
with that knowledge, he tries to figure out how to minimize the bad consequences of human action and maximize the good.

The basic commandment of this approach, with
which I agree, is that voluntary transactions are presumptively preferred because they are positive-sum
games from which both sides benefit. In contrast, the
use of fraud and coercion are regarded with deep sus-
picion because these are pure transfer games in which
one side may benefit (somewhat) and the other side will
lose (a great deal more). We need some way to net out
the pluses and the minuses of coercive transactions. On
this score, the somber conclusion is that the minuses
are likely to dominate simply because people are less
likely to resort to theft when they can organize a voluntary transaction that works to their mutual advantage.
When people resort to force and deception, they surely

pay a price, but it is likely to be far lower than the harm they inflict on others whose lives, limbs, and fortunes are placed at risk. On these critical points, the insights of libertarian theory cannot be ignored, even if they may have to be qualified.

The second point that the libertarian rightly grasps is that one good idea—voluntary exchange—applied multiple times becomes a truly great idea. If law sets up a system in which two people make a transaction, then each can take what he receives in any given exchange and decide to consume it, invest it, or resell it to a third person. The more rapid the velocity of transactions, the more likely that all individuals will exhaust the full set of gains available from the contractual process. Mutual gain is therefore piled on top of mutual gain in transactions that involve two or more persons. In seeking to understand private contracts, it is always a mistake to think of them as one-shot transactions in a stagnant economy. Rather, it is a dynamic system in which the ceaseless exchange of goods and services generates positive consequences for other people whose opportunities are enhanced by the greater wealth and prosperity of their neighbors. The point is that a system of private property and voluntary exchange does produce a fair share of externalities, but to the extent that these are routinely positive, not negative, the externalities give truth to the old proposition of the late John F. Kennedy—a rising tide raises all ships. Quite simply, so long as all individuals can participate in the operation of a market system, no tiny group of individuals will be able

to corner the wealth—and through it, the well-being—
that it generates.

Unlike the model of socialism, the libertarian position has positive features that must be incorporated in
any more comprehensive view of the world. The libertarian model comports so well with our ordinary expe-
riential base that it is easy—almost too easy—to think
that it offers the full solution to our social problem. After
all, there is much to be said for a system that allows
complex social organizations—commercial, social, and
charitable—to arise out of a sequence of voluntary transactions that recombine initial endowments of property
and labor in packages that work to the long-term advantage of all their participants. The point of vulnerability
of this system, however, is that it cannot generate from
its own motion the background social conditions that
allow it to flourish. A system of property rights requires
the enforcement of the boundaries that keep persons
apart. Self-help is one possible solution to this problem,
but it is a mantle that can be claimed by aggressors as
well as by their victims. Self-declarations will not allow
us to sort out these two groups from each other. Nor
will it be easy to find a market solution to this problem,
because every side to a dispute (many of which involve
more than two individuals) will demand some control
over the choice of the final referee. It is because of this
void that we have the need for (and fear of) a single
institution that makes authoritative decisions about the
rights and duties of the various individuals and firms
within a complex society. We thus find ourselves in the
unhappy situation of demanding some sort of state mo-

nopoly to enforce the rights that make a decentralized economic system possible. Indeed, the ambiguities go deeper than all this, for voluntary transactions and private property take place on top of a social infrastructure that no market can supply.

On this point, I am always impressed by market-oriented writers, such as Hernando DeSoto (1989, 2000), who start with the social necessity of having single state-run systems for market economies to flourish. DeSoto's simplest example was that of ordinary street addresses, without which it is not possible to organize a system for delivering the mail or supplying electricity, gas, police, and fire services. This simple commitment to a legal and physical infrastructure requires a system of public taxation and finance. These institutions cannot operate strictly and solely on voluntary cooperation, because virtually all (self-interested) individuals will have a tendency to let others pick up the lion's share of the cost from the collective institutions from which they hope to benefit (see, for example, Olson [1965]). Public-spirited individuals are too few and far between to pick up the slack. Unfortunately, everyone cannot stand back from collective responsibilities in the vain hope that necessary public services will somehow be supplied by others. Hence, the great challenge in liberal democracies is to figure out how to use systems of coercion to benefit the very individuals and institutions subjected to them. Stated otherwise, the public provision of any goods and services necessarily presupposes a system of public taxation and finance. For these funds to be spent intelligently, we need to develop a sound collective judgment as to which infrastructure projects are worth undertaking and which are not. If the libertarian holds fast to the assumption that all forms of state coercion are equal, then he strips himself of the tools that might allow him to segregate those state projects that are worth doing from those that are not. Likewise, the rejection of all systems of taxation makes it impossible to distinguish between better and worse systems of taxation and exposes a serious political theory to the most dangerous of refutations—ridicule.

There is a bright side, however. Once we recognize that private markets need these public systems, we can at least develop a criterion by which we should judge the public use of force: does the use of coercion benefit those who are subject to the taxes and regulation that government imposes? Stated in a single sentence, the key weakness of the hard libertarian position is that it does not make room for situations where property is, and ought to be, taken—be it by occupation, regulation, or taxation—in exchange for just compensation—be it in cash or in the form of in-kind benefits, such as the increased security of private property and voluntary transactions. This immense area of forced exchanges does not concede an "open sesame" to state power. Rather, it is hemmed in with serious limitations on what state actions may be undertaken, and toward what end, and what forms of compensation should be supplied. I have written of these subjects at great length elsewhere (Epstein, 1985; Epstein, 1993). Suffice it to say, it is possible to devise rules that permit the provision of needed public goods without allowing the state to succumb to political favoritism that leads to massive transfers of wealth from one political faction to another. The candid response to the challenge of forced exchanges to the provision of public (i.e., nondivisible and nonexclusive) goods is what the standard libertarian theory most critically lacks. It is for this reason that I often prefer the label "classical liberal," on the ground that the basic theory recognizes the need for some government role in supplying public good that libertarians may acknowledge but that their stripped-down theories cannot fully explain.

COMPETITIVE MARKETS AND
COMPENSATION FOR COMPETITIVE HARMS

Rather than pursue this thorny topic here, I am approaching this lecture in a more simpleminded mood. Because I want to address the easy cases that do not depend on the complex conceptions of public goods and just compensation, which play so large a role in markets such as transportation and communication, the differences between the libertarian and the classical liberal are, for this exercise at least, relatively unimportant. More concretely, my objective is to return to those many markets where we do not have to worry about these massive coordination problems precisely because two individuals can enter into exchanges that promote their mutual gain even if they are unable to secure the cooperation or participation of anyone else. Where then does the simple logic of voluntary contracting lead us in this connection?

Clearly, this world is not devoid of problems. In any exchange between two persons, it is important to ask whether it is truly voluntary or whether it is subject to duress, fraud, or some other form of undue influence. This will certainly be an issue in transactions that involve medical treatment for old or infirm persons whose cognitive capacities are sharply limited. Indeed, much of the debate in medical ethics relates to the question of what should be done in situations where people are, at best, marginally competent to make critical decisions about their own future. But the concerns that permeate certain specialized transactions are, thankfully, not a serious concern in most organized markets. Undue influence is not a real issue in mercantile transactions that take place on open exchanges. These trades usually work just as the textbook says they should: they produce benefits to the two traders, which in turn sets up opportunities for a third person to profit as well. So, the basic situation leaves us in the best of all possible worlds, where a local improvement between two parties is accompanied by a generalized form of social improvement. But it is here that our difficulties begin, for any successful trade may often leave in its wake one or more disappointed competitors who are worse off in this particular instance because of their inability to make the sale. Their competitive loss is a real economic harm, and it is always possible for individuals to ignore the systematic gains from trade and insist that they should receive some sort of compensation for their competitive loss.

It is on this big, easy question that the rubber hits

the road, for anyone who is committed to the classical liberal position will fight to the death against the compensation for losses arising in a competitive economy, notwithstanding the fierce resistance routinely encountered in practice. The common argument is that economic losses from competition are every bit as real to their victims as those that result from the use of force. If we allow compensation for physical injuries and injunctions against their future occurrence, then we should do the same for competitive losses, which should likewise be enjoined or compensated.

As I noted earlier, the classical writers on this subject rejected these claims with a Latin phrase, *damnum absque ininuria*, which translated means "harm without injury," or, as lawyers would say today, "harm but not actionable harm." Clearly, the use of this Latin expression smacks of the argument by fiat to which I referred earlier. It is important to note that we can develop a more systematic, theoretical argument against this claim for protection from or compensation for competitive losses, which runs as follows. There is a world of *social* difference between the harms inflicted by the use of force and those inflicted through competition. In the first case, we know that injury to the person and damage to property reduces the total store of resources available for human betterment. One person, to make himself better off, inflicts the losses on a second person. That individual's reduced stock of wealth necessarily reduces the opportunities for trade that are available to third persons. The externalities from coercion turn from generally positive to sharply *negative*. However much a single actor might benefit from his own use of force, no one thinks it is possible to prosper in a society that generalizes from that experience and that allows all individuals to adopt the same practices at will.

In contrast, competition may cause harm to one rival producer, but it also leaves his stock of labor and capital intact for a second transaction. By helping trading partners, it opens up new avenues to those individuals who receive goods at low prices and of high quality and to the many third persons who stand to benefit in further transactions. To take a broad definition of actionable harm transforms liability from an occasional occurrence, such as a car accident, into an inevitable and ubiquitous occurrence: If A's success in competition is an actionable harm to B, then so too is B's success to A. A's claim only looks plausible when considered in isolation; it looks grotesque when its full implications are considered.

Here is not the place to repeat the demonstrations that competitive markets maximize welfare by exhausting the gains from trade. It is quite enough to say that compensation for or protection from competitive losses destroys the gains from trade at every juncture. It may well be that the disappointed trader loses more from competition than from petty theft. But from a larger point of view, competition as a process produces systematic social gains, while coercion and force as a process produce systematic social losses. The willingness to protect individuals against physical loss to person or property, or against defamation and other forms of molestation that involve either misrepresentation or threats of force, has the great virtue of allowing individual lawsuits to go forward when private and social welfare are perfectly aligned. But any offer of compensation or other protection to the disappointed trader has exactly the opposite effect: it places a giant wedge between individual and social welfare. The point here does not depend on the particulars of the product or service offered. It is not undermined by the most painful stories novelists can write about the havoc that demonic competition imposes on those who have found themselves displaced by market forces. It is a general proposition that is capable of general affirmation. It is one of those easy cases that it is absolutely vital to get correct: *there must be no compensation or protection against economic losses sustained through the operation of competitive markets*. It is a principle that is widely acknowledged and violated in practice.

3. Competition and Cartels

To show the power of this general proposition, I will examine in greater detail two types of critical markets in which a strong political will could preserve the operation of competitive markets. These markets are agriculture and labor. In both cases, the question of competitive harm has played an enormous role in shaping the legal rules that govern them. In both cases, it is easy to envisage a competitive solution in which parties are able to buy and sell commodities and labor on whatever terms and conditions they see fit. In neither case do we have to worry about the need to create social infrastructure or to assemble complex networks through the wise use of government coercion. All that is needed is a willingness to allow prices to move in accordance with principles of supply and demand and to limit the use of monopoly power on either side of the market. This could be accomplished by a modest antitrust or competition policy that focuses on horizontal arrangements to limit quantity or to raise price. To be sure, the antitrust solution does not have an obvious libertarian pedigree, for it does not conform to the libertarian belief that the content of a contract is solely the business of the parties to it and not the concern of any third person. In contrast, a classical liberal will share Adam Smith's distaste for monopoly and will distinguish sharply between monopoly and competition (see *The Wealth of Nations*, 1776). The classical liberal recognizes the social dislocations produced by the former condition, when prices are raised above marginal costs and fewer goods and services are produced than in a competitive system. This bad result can be achieved when a single firm produces all the goods and services in a particular market or when rival producers are able to organize themselves into a cartel, so that their production and pricing decisions replicate those of the single firm with monopoly power.

The social losses that flow from monopolies or cartels are capable of identification by economic theory, so that the central question is whether the tools that could be used to counter their effects are reliable enough to justify the costs of their imposition. In the traditional English system, these contracts to rig markets were not enforceable among the parties to them. The lack of state enforcement fostered a strong tendency to "cheat" among cartel members, which tended to bring prices back to competitive levels. After all, each member of the cartel would do very well if it chiseled a bit on price so long as all the other members kept to the higher price. But once any individual seller cuts his prices, the others would be sure to follow suit until the entire system fell under its own weight. The downward pressure would be further exacerbated if new firms were allowed to enter the market under the price umbrella that the cartel created. In essence, the minimalist strategy to deal with cartels is two-pronged. First, deny enforcement of any agreement among cartel members, and, second, allow new entry, so that the entire system will sooner or later fall under its own weight. The more aggressive critique of this position is that this low-key approach will allow cartels to operate, and perhaps even to thrive, for limited periods of time. Their gains could be prolonged, moreover, if the rival firms merged, because a unified operation would no longer have to worry about cheating by any of its members. Thus, the more aggressive strategy imposes sanctions on cartels, both civil and criminal, and allows the state to block mergers that operate, as the expression goes, in restraint of trade.

For these purposes, I do not wish to take sides on whether the more aggressive arm of competition policy has borne fruit. Much depends on whether the enforcement of these competition laws turns out to be misguided, so that it punishes firms that aggressively compete for business on the ground that they are engaged in some unlawful form of "predation." Much also depends on whether the evidentiary rules that are used to isolate cartels and cooperative agreements are sensibly enforced. If they allow too much collusive behavior to slip through the net, then the system of antitrust regulation is not worth its cost. If these rules catch, by mistake, too much procompetitive behavior, then the edifice turns out to be counterproductive. Resolving these questions raises a host of hard trade-offs that I shall avoid, consistent with the theme of this lecture. What is striking, however, is how the development of agricultural and labor markets proceed from quite different assumptions.

The law in both countries has done a total flip-flop on the question of legality. Far from condemning cartels, it has worked overtime to prop them up precisely because it sees competitive harm as something to be feared, not welcomed. Starting from that position, the law helps cartels by systematically countering the two risks to which any collusive arrangement is subject: the inability to police the conduct of its own members against cheating and the inability to block the entrance of new firms that bring matters back to the competitive equilibrium. We may have some uneasiness about the use of state power to enforce a competition policy directed against private collusive agreements, but whatever the doubts on that score, in principle, we have no reason to reverse the policy in so dramatic a fashion in the two key areas of agriculture and labor policy. My greater expertise on these areas is chiefly with the U.S. sources, but I shall refer to analogous British experiences to show that this dangerous tendency has truly international appeal, both historically and in the present day.

At this point, we have to ask why the forces within the agricultural and labor sectors were able to obtain that extraordinary dispensation from the state. Part of the explanation is technical. It is a sad but powerful truth that those markets that work best under perfect competition are also the ones that offer the greatest opportunities for cartelization. Fungible products are helpful for creating competitive markets. Once products are standardized, it is far easier to have a large number of buyers and sellers in the market because the standardization of products leads to an ease of comparison and substitution—the hallmarks of competitive markets. Thus, the ability to organize work in mass-production facilities creates opportunities for competitive labor markets as does the standardization of agricultural produce.

Unfortunately, the flip side of the proposition is every bit as potent. The standardization that allows for the emergence of competitive markets also paves the way for the formation of cartels, by both public and private means. So long as all sellers and workers are delivering the same product, it is easier for the cartel to coordinate prices and collateral terms. In contrast, in markets that feature highly individualized products, such as distinctive parcels of real estate, invariably there will be some jockeying over prices. The nonstandard nature of the good creates a spread between the maximum amount the buyer will pay and the minimum amount the seller will expect. Accordingly, the parties will have to bargain out those differences. We need to live with friction in ordinary transactions even if we never learn to love it. Now, when you have perfectly standardized goods, all of this tends to disappear because of the ability to find a perfect substitute by going next door in a business district that specializes in the same kind of commodity. The full information that makes competition possible in standardized goods is exactly the same condition that makes collusion work. If every seller knows that the rival sellers are selling exactly the same good that he is and for exactly the same price, the gains to organizing this particular market to cut back production and raise prices (or wages) will make the privileged group better off and the rest of the world worse off. First, they have to pay for this elaborate scheme to the extent that it is subsidized by tax revenues; and second, they now have to pay a monopolistic price or wage that is higher than the competitive one. Additional complications will arise when price discrimination is available. But in our current reductionist frame of mind, it is best to put these to one side. The upshot is that we should see the greatest efforts at collusion in those markets that are most amenable to competitive solutions.

A moment's reflection, however, should show that these points are not sufficient to explain why the organizers of agricultural and labor markets were able to gain state support for their endeavors when ordinary manufacturers were subject to increased scrutiny of their behavior. So much turns on the intellectual climate of opinion in which the legislative and judicial deliberations take place. Any political body contains many members who do not have a large stake on either side of the question. These people are neither agricultural producers nor agricultural consumers; they are neither employers nor workers, at least in the first instance. The ability to sway these neutral groups in argument often proves critical in gaining the necessary level of political support. The reason people on all sides of the political spectrum are to this day so concerned with forums like these, in which ideas are discussed and debated, is that they know that their political influence will only take them so far. If the public sentiment is strongly stacked against them, their options are limited. But if the political climate is congenial to their industry agenda, then their chances of political success correspondingly rise.

It is against this background that we can understand why appeals of farmers and workers could gain success while those of industrialists are turned aside because of, not in spite of, their greater wealth. Never underestimate the enhanced political sympathy when the underdog seeks to gain state power. Neither workers nor (individual) farmers are at the top of the income distribution, so they are perceived as having to struggle against greater powers on the other side of the market. In some cases, there may be a point here—for example, if railways are able to collude to raise the freight costs of shipping goods, some might argue in favor of creating a countervailing monopoly power for those that suffer.[1] However, in this situation the proper solution is to break up the initial collusion, not to create a rival monopoly that will be at loggerheads with the original one. But so long as people see the struggle between farmer and railways or capital and labor as a zero-sum game in which one side, by definition, wins what the other side loses, then it is easy to make the underdogs favorites in the game of life.

But once it is realized that this simplified view of the world omits some key concerns, then the persuasiveness of this maudlin plea should diminish. Successful cartelization by any group hurts not only their immediate purchasers but also all the others who, in turn, purchase from them, including ordinary consumers who

1. The buying power of supermarkets might be a corresponding example relevant to the United Kingdom (Wood, this volume).

may be more down on their luck than the individual cartel members. In addition, the entire process is never a simple transfer of wealth from one side to the other; instead, it is part of an elaborate process that results in the systematic destruction of wealth from at least three sources: the creation of an inferior market structure, the political costs needed to put that structure in place, and the nontrivial administrative costs to make sure that the program does not fall apart. At this point it does not make a difference whether the popular political forces are heard in Westminster, Brussels, or Washington. They all sing the same tune about the simple distributive consequences of cartel formation that overlooks the long-term consequences of these arrangements. One cannot rectify the problems arising from an undesired distribution of income or bargaining power by creating more cartels, such as those in agricultural and labor markets.

4. Agricultural Markets, Protectionism, and Cartels

A RIGHT TO FARM?

I think that this general analysis is borne out by a closer look at the agricultural and labor markets. Let me start with the American agricultural market in an effort to see how it learned to deal with the uncertainties introduced by fierce competition in a setting where technical progress tended to increase output and, therefore, to reduce prices. Individual farmers knew they could not alter that outcome by individual actions, for the laws of competition mete out harsh penalties on sellers who do not meet the competitive price. Raise prices and you lose your customer base; lower prices and you lose your profits. No wonder *everyone* wants public dispensation from competition. Indeed, in agriculture, if it is allowed to run without state intervention, then rising productivity should lead to an exit of farmers from the market. This exit is welcomed from a social perspective because it releases valuable resources for other more valued uses, but it is clearly not welcomed from the perspective of individual farmers.

Yet one of the great political successes of the agricultural movement is that it sought to insulate its members from the uncertainties of price fluctuations by appealing to the so-called parity principle, by which farmers sought to maintain prices at the constant high levels, relative to other goods, that they were able to fetch in the bumper years between 1910 and 1914. There is no question that fixed prices make life easier for farmers, but they make it far more difficult for everyone else who has to bear the full brunt of any fluctuation in supply and demand. The government has to use taxpayers' money to enter the market to soak up the excess demand, or it must find a way to reduce the level of production so as to maintain the prices at the desired level. Clearly strong subsidies and restrictions are needed to meet this unwarranted goal.

How is it, then, that any group is able to insulate itself from world uncertainties when that form of protection increases the uncertainty for everyone else? Part of the solution is rhetorical, with a strong appeal to positive rights. Thus, when Franklin Roosevelt introduced his second bill of rights on economic matters in his 1944 State of the Union address, the constant theme of "the right to farm" was very prominent on his list and helped pave the way for the post–World War II dominance by the farm lobby on agricultural policy. But what is meant by "a right to farm"? As an analytical matter, every assertion of a right should give rise to an instant query as to its correlative duty. Here, the claim of a right to farm has to be set against two different kinds of correlative duties with vastly different implications. The first of the duties is that if somebody has the right to farm, nobody can block that person's entry or exit from the business. Hence, any farmers can offer produce for sale at whatever price to whomever they see fit, so long as they can find a willing buyer. So, the right to farm reduces to a particular application of the more general right to go into any lawful occupation; entry and pricing decisions are left to the individual alone. Deals, however, require a willing buyer. If that were all that was involved, then the agricultural lobby would simply be working fiercely for free competition and open markets. Who could complain?

Of course, that proposition is not what they mean when farmers claim the right to farm. What they mean is that once they enter a particular occupation, they have a right to remain in that occupation, no matter what the conditions or what changes in demand or supply take place. At this point, the government's position or obligation is to make sure that any farmer can persevere as a farmer so long as he desires to remain in the trade. Major steps are taken to insulate farmers from the powerful economic forces that engulf everyone else.

AGRICULTURE AS AN EASY CASE

The system, however, requires not only rhetoric but also specific economic measures to sustain it. Here, in effect, we find an inversion of the three central principles that organize economic markets: restraint of trade is now allowed, entry of new firms is blocked, and massive subsidies are used to prop up the overall arrangement. Easy questions, big errors. Here is a thumbnail sketch of how it all works.

One way to raise prices is to enter into contracts in restraint of trade. In principle, every single contract between two rival sellers could be treated as a restraint of trade, for it reduces the number of sellers from 1000 to 999. But the key point here is not to deny that some small restraint in trade has happened, for indeed it has. It is important to stress the smallness of that effect, for given this change in market structure, none of the remaining 999 firms obtains any real market power to set price or curtail output. Indeed, even this small change in market structure is likely to prove a nonevent if a new firm takes up where an old one left off. Contracts in restraint of trade only start to bite when the level of collusion is high enough for the few independent pricing decisions to allow sellers to raise market prices. But the formation of a firm has a second effect that is much more powerful. It allows for division of labor and a specialization of effort within the firm that makes this new operation a much more formidable competitor than the sole trader who has none of these advantages. The point here, moreover, neatly generalizes because the system becomes better if everyone forms more efficient firms, at least until the concentration becomes so high that the balance of advantage shifts. The gains from specialization are not likely to continue as firms become ever larger, but the risk of monopolization grows. Therefore, we have to adopt some rule of reason that sets the "horizontal" transaction against a backdrop of general economic theory from which we could conclude that 100 strong and efficient firms will do better than a marketplace of 1000 underdeveloped ones. The world is full of trade-offs, even on questions of merger.

Much of this learning has to crystallize around the

phrase "contract in restraint of trade," which will cover the giant trust but not the two-man firm. In the United States, the Sherman Act of 1890 marked the first federal effort to place a generalized prohibition on private efforts to monopolize various markets, and its reach was extended by the Clayton Act of 1914, which was passed under the "progressive" influences in the early days of the Wilson administration. Here, it is instructive to set out the Act's terms for two reasons. First, it illustrates the close connection between labor and agricultural markets in the regulatory framework. Second, it shows the dangerous inversion of classical liberal principles, not because there is error on a hard question but because it gets the easy questions wrong in principle. Here is the text of Section 6 of the Clayton Act:

> The labor of a human being is not a commodity or article of commerce. Nothing contained in the antitrust laws shall be construed to forbid the existence and operation of labor, agricultural, or horticultural organizations, instituted for the purposes of mutual help, and not having capital stock or conducted for profit, or forbid or restrain individual members of such organizations from lawfully carrying out the legitimate objects thereof; nor shall such organizations, or the members thereof, be held or construed to be illegal combinations or conspiracies in restraint of trade, under the antitrust laws.

This passage is rich in rhetorical power and symbolism. On the first point, the initial sentence only refers to "the labor of a human being"—to which we shall return—because even the most ardent defender of cartels could not claim that agricultural produce did not count as a commodity or an article of commerce. But the consequences are the same nonetheless. Both labor and agricultural organizations are, in so many terms, exempted from the class of contracts in restraint of trade that run afoul of the antitrust laws. The powerful differences among types of contracts prove to be of critical importance, as this provision remains in force to this very day. Indeed, the same spirit that informs this section of the Clayton Act also influences the interpretation of the general Sherman Act prohibition against cartels and other contracts in restraint of trade. Where various groups who are not protected by the Clayton Act have worked to obtain the assistance of state governments in organizing cartels for their produce sales, the question is whether this activity is caught by the Sherman Act. At the height of the New Deal, the answer to this question was "no," in the important 1943 case of *Parker v. Brown*. This case held that the decision of California to organize a raisin cartel for sales to citizens mainly in other states was immunized from antitrust scrutiny because the Sherman Act was, in the first instance, only directed toward private cartels.

The *Parker* decision is remarkable for two reasons. First, the system in question misses the critical point that state-sponsored cartels are more dangerous than private ones precisely because the state enforcement reduces the (desirable) possibility of cheating by its members. Second, in this case, the brunt of the high prices was borne by individuals and firms that lived or operated in other states. This was a case in which California was able to export misery elsewhere, just as the general blessing of export cartels in the United States under the Webb-Pomereine Act also places smaller amounts of domestic gain ahead of larger amounts of foreign dislocation. The political economy point could not be clearer: today, the question of whether cartels are good or bad should be determined on a case-by-case basis. Yet no reason is offered as to why some cartels should flourish and others not. The strong classical liberal tradition may have doubts about breaking up voluntary cartels for fear its efforts could misfire, but this should offer no consolation to those who wish to prop them up with state power, as is done here. In any event, it is clear that in agricultural markets, American domestic policy sweeps aside any principled objection to state-sponsored cartels.

The next question is whether this strategy will succeed. The basic answer is that an exemption from competition law, without more, would be most imperfect. There are two reasons for this. First, other firms could still enter the market under the umbrella that the cartel's price list broadcasts to the rest of the world. Given sufficient numbers, new entrants would bid down prices to the competitive level. Second, individual members could expand their output in ways that could escape detection, although this is less of a threat, obviously, when public funds are used to monitor the behavior of cartel members. The next inversion of classical liberal principle, therefore, is that the incumbents must be able to choke off new entry and to make sure that the individual farmers still in business do not expand their production in ways that drive down the price. There are a number of techniques that help achieve this situation: acreage restrictions, for example, could limit the number of acres that individual farmers could place under cultivation. Or bumper crops could be purchased by government officials, again with the view of restricting the supply that reaches the market. The agricultural marketing order thus becomes the tool of choice to restrain supply.

Within the American context, however, this task was not easily done before and during the New Deal because of the constitutional impediments that arguably stood in the way of any administrative system of production restraints. The original design gave the U.S. government only limited powers, the most expansive of which was the so-called commerce power, which provided that Congress has the power "to regulate commerce with foreign nations, among the several states, and with the Indian tribes" (U.S. Constitution, Art. I, §8). The traditional view of that power was that it allowed Congress to regulate the shipment of goods and people across state lines, but it did not allow for the regulation of agriculture or manufacture, all of which took place within the individual states. The grant of the commerce power was intended chiefly to make sure that Congress could neutralize the barriers to commerce that individual states might wish to create in order to protect their own manufacturers and farmers from out-of-state competition. But the language of the clause was not perfectly congruent with that end, because the affirmative power to regulate commerce could be turned to restrictive ends, as frequently happened with the protective tariffs that were passed under the aegis of the foreign commerce power.

On this score, one of the unanticipated developments in constitutional doctrine involved the judicial creation of the *dormant*, or *negative*, commerce clause, which said that the case for a national common market was so strong that states could not frustrate its operations in the absence of clear authorization from Congress. No state can stop your transports or your telephone wires from running across their boundary line. The upshot was that the Supreme Court took it upon itself to police the actions of the various states. Ironically, the doctrinal pedigree of the dormant commerce clause was far from secure, for an explicit grant of power to Congress does not automatically translate into an implicit limitation on the power of the states. But if we put those interpretive issues to one side, for the most part, the U.S. Supreme Court has done a decent, indeed near admirable, job in keeping the lines of commerce clear while allowing the states, on clear and convincing evidence, to limit the importation of goods when they could establish a paramount local interest in health and safety, narrowly defined. The point here is that because the Court has shown a deep and consistent commitment to competition across state boundaries, it has worked hard to see that the needed accommodations have been made, and it has refused to defer to clever ruses that advance the cause of protectionism under such dubious banners as the ostensible indirect health and safety benefits from price stabilization. Much of the engine of U.S. economic growth can be traced to this one heroic judicial innovation, for Congress has, on most occasions, been slow to overturn state legislation that the Supreme Court has struck down. The federal system works when Congress is silent, and the synthesis that has been created under the dormant commerce clause is an appropriate model for the program of the World Trade Organization or the European Union today.

CHANGES IN THE ATTITUDE OF CONGRESS IN THE 1930S

The dormant commerce clause, however, is not the dominant part of the American story. Rather, the key developments of the modern welfare state involve the radical expansion of the affirmative commerce power. The basic decisions to cast aside the traditional limitations on congressional power came just after the court-packing crisis of 1937, when the Supreme Court switched course and held that Congress could regulate agriculture and manufacturing, to the extent that the industries had, as they always do, an indirect economic effect on the national economy. Once the floodgates were open, Congress responded in predictable fashion, and the dislocations of the 1930s were largely attributable to two catastrophic mistakes. The first was the Smoot-Hawley tariff, a form of protectionism, which, as noted, fell squarely within the scope of the foreign commerce power. Regrettably, it was designed to allow for the creation of a tariff wall around the United States. The second was the steep deflation that increased the real debt of farmers and others by an unanticipated manipulation of the currency. In turn, it led to massive foreclosures and other dislocations, many of which preceded Franklin Roosevelt's rise to the presidency in 1933.

But little effort was made to attack these two causes of economic woe directly. Rather, in connection with agriculture, the effort was focused on creating a nationwide cartel for agricultural produce, which did nothing to address the underlying structural difficulties but only exacerbated the whole situation by adding a third set of mistaken programs to the witch's brew. The cartelization effort could not be achieved by the individual states acting on their own, for the importation of produce across state lines effectively undermined local efforts to rig the market. Nor could cartelization be accomplished by the national government under the restricted view of the commerce power, because in-state sales and home consumption of farm goods could undercut the restrictive effects of any national order. But at this point, the U.S. Supreme Court had lost its basic faith in markets and, thus, could see no reason to restrict the power of Congress in an integrated national economy to attack these local sales and consumptions. As the marketing orders from the U.S. Department of Agriculture went out, the Court, in rapid succession, first sustained the power of the federal government to regulate in-state sales of milk, which were undertaken in competition with milk marketed on an interstate basis (*U.S. v. Wrightwood*); next, in what has to be regarded as a tour de force of constitutional interpretation, the court held that Congress could regulate the feeding of grain to one's own cows under the commerce power even when there was no commercial transaction, state or interstate, at all (*Wickard v. Filburn*). In a weird sense, its logic was unassailable: any leak in the restrictive wall would undercut the overall power of the cartel, so the power of Congress to move had to follow the threats, even if these activities were as "local" as one could imagine. And local consumption of grains could consume as much, I am told, as 20 or 25 percent of local production. There is little exaggeration to say that the expansion of federal power in the United States, as far as agriculture is concerned, was to make the world safe for cartels.

In the pre–New Deal era, the judicial resistance to state-sponsored cartels was manifest in yet another doctrine with clear English origins. To backtrack for a moment, the basic English position was that the owner of property could normally charge what the market would bear, where the clear implication was that competition by rival sellers would place an effective check on price. But at the same time, the English courts, following the lead of Sir Matthew Hale, took the position that the state could regulate the prices in those industries that were "affected with the public interest." Those firms that had, either by virtue of government grant or natural advantage, a monopoly position were the prime targets of this prohibition. Hale's position was relied on extensively in the 1810 English decision in *Allnut v. Inglis*, where it was held that the operator of a Crown custom house, in which goods were stored for shipment overseas free of customs duties, could only charge a reasonable rate; otherwise, the increment in price could largely nullify the tax break that had been supplied by the Crown. *Allnut* made its way into American constitutional law in the post–Civil War period, where it was used in far more complex settings to allow the state to limit the rate of return that could be charged by the natural monopolies in the network industries that emerged in the last third of the nineteenth century. Once again, there are many difficult questions on the permissible forms of state regulation: after all, if rates are set too high, then the monopoly can prosper, but if they are set too low, then the individual owners of the venture would not be able to recover a reasonable rate of return on their investments.

SUBSIDIES, TARIFFS, AND PROTECTION

As befits the temper of this lecture, I shall not stop to explain the ins and outs of the American doctrine. Instead, I shall turn again to the easy cases gone wrong. Somewhat oversimplified, the basic position of pre–New Deal American constitutionalism was that the states and national government had substantial power to combat the dangers of monopoly, but none to regulate the prices and rates that could be charged in competitive markets. This made good economic sense. Any effort to reduce the rates of competitive firms would, in effect, drive them into bankruptcy or confiscate their wealth. Any effort to increase their prices and rates would cartelize a competitive industry. The public loses either way if it is forced to spend resources on regulation in order to obtain an inferior outcome. But this sensible constitu-

tional synthesis gave way in 1934 in *Nebbia v. New York*
when the Supreme Court, on matters of rate regulation,
showed the same degree of agnosticism toward this doctrine that it was to show shortly thereafter toward the
commerce clause. It is no surprise that the transformation in doctrine was done with an eye to allowing the
state of New York to make it a crime to sell milk to
consumers at less than nine cents per quart. A doctrine
that had been designed to curb the power of monopolies
and cartels was now reinvented to permit the state to
strengthen their hand. It is again critical to realize just
how much of American constitutional doctrine has been
driven to make the world safe for cartels.

I have less to say about the third part of the inversion. As a matter of basic principle, the appropriate cases
for subsidy are limited to those activities that generate
some kind of public (or nonexcludable) benefit for the
community at large. Otherwise, subsidies, in their own
way, distort competitive markets as much as restrictions
on output do. The individuals who bear only some portion of the cost of production will continue to produce
goods until their private marginal cost equals their private return. That private decision will, however, yield
systematic overproduction of goods, because the additional public moneys spent do not generate social gains
of equal value. The net effect is too many goods for too
high a social price. The situation gets worse in the long
run, as the firms that do not make an orderly exit before
the subsidy is supplied continue to press for its expansion long after it has been put in place. I wish I could
report that there were a series of American constitutional

doctrines that sought to limit the ability of the state and national governments to supply subsidies to what should otherwise be competitive industries, but the sad truth is that, as the constant wrangling in the World Trade Organization shows, it is a lot harder to define a subsidy than it is to define a restraint of trade and harder to regulate subsidies, even when they amount to direct subventions for the production of particular goods. For example, can we determine objectively whether providing good roads in agricultural areas is a subsidy to agricultural products? The constitutional history inside the United States is therefore much like the toleration of subsidies encountered elsewhere. Political forces turn out to be regnant, and all too often they interact with tariffs and the domestic situation to produce a most ungodly situation.

I have no deep knowledge of the British or the European Union tradition, but I have no doubt that the forces that have proved so powerful within the American context have manifested themselves on the other side of the Atlantic. There is, of course, no tradition of judicial review that might have placed brakes on legislative power, but the fundamentals are the same. The only way the cartels can operate is by the restriction of entry, which means high tariff walls and powerful systems of national allocation. And any group that is powerful enough to organize protection can usually gain some direct or indirect subsidy. It takes only a peek at the current newspapers to realize that this free trade issue will not go away, whether it is manifested through debates over genetically modified foods in the European

Union or the U.S. steel tariff, mercifully lifted by the president only after it allowed economic wounds to fester for the better part of two years. It is a testament to the defect of our political institutions that positions that have so little to commend them intellectually are able to gain such political mileage.

Why, one might ask, do we see this regrettable set of results? I do not believe it stems from any conceptual inability to perceive the dangers of protectionism in the abstract. The case against mercantilism and protection is one of the great achievements of Adam Smith's *Wealth of Nations*, which does not grow dim from repetition. But even if we put aside the emotional appeals made by discrete and identifiable groups that lose from competition, there is still another reason for the regrettable persistence of restraints in international trade: it is the problem of the second best. We can all agree that if all nations were to lift all trade barriers, all would benefit from the result. But what if the local faction of farmers in one nation or bloc captures the levers of power, and a similar phenomenon takes place elsewhere, perhaps dominated by the steel industry or owners of intellectual property? Here the issue of path dependence becomes paramount. Each side will demand liberalization from the other before it is prepared to take the first step of its own. The interconnections between intellectual property and agriculture have been apparent in the international arena since the World Trade Organization Doha round of talks, and the recent shipwreck in Cancún shows just how difficult these struggles are.

UNILATERAL REFORM WOULD BRING BIG GAINS

But even so, there should be a clear course of action: declare unilateral surrender. The use of agricultural subsidies and trade barriers causes huge domestic dislocations. The United States, for example, would be far better off in its own economic well-being if it scrapped these programs tomorrow, even if the rest of the world were determined to keep them in place. We could get the benefit of more goods and services in the United States, including those that are foolishly subsidized by foreign governments. We win, no matter what the rest of the world does. In this regard, it is useful to recall the great contribution of David Ricardo, who pointed out that the nation that imposes tariffs on imports hurts itself in the export market even if it invites no retaliation from abroad. The simple but ingenious point is that the relative value of the two currencies will not remain the same once the tariff is imposed. The shrinking demand for goods from abroad reduces the demand for the currency in which those goods are sold. The local currency thus becomes more expensive relative to the foreign currency, which acts as a price barrier to export. That cost is effectively avoided by a unilateral policy on free trade.

In looking at the wreckage of U.S., EU, and world politics in agriculture, it is important to ask just how much protectionism matters. In one sense, it matters less than meets the eye. Determining what goods are made available is a function not only of the political organization that surrounds their sale, but also of the cost of production and the quality of the goods so produced.

The raw products are only part of the overall price, and the incredible improvements in efficiency have driven down world prices so that the self-interested cartelist will find it in its interest to lower prices to maximize profits. The numbers here are huge: an egg costs about 5 percent of what it did 100 years ago because of the ceaseless innovation at every stage of production, much of which takes place in ways that the agricultural cartel cannot identify, let alone reach. But before we rejoice in our good fortune, note that the gains from technology are not spread uniformly around the world, and in some contexts they do little to offset the advantages of climate and cheap labor found in less-developed parts of the world. What has caused minor dislocations in advanced nations could wreak devastation in backward economies that can only expand if they gain access to developed markets. Then again, this is one consistent cost of regulation. Democracy works on a territorial principle, such that those who do not vote do not really count, even if they suffer. What for us are small issues, are for others matters of life and death.

5. Cartels in Labor Markets

LET US NOW TURN to the labor market. To most people, any purported connection between labor and agricultural markets will be dismissed as fanciful. They don't seem to have very much in common. But initial appearances can mislead. First, the two are linked in Section 6 of the Clayton Act, which at the very least suggests that there was an alliance between labor and agricultural movements. Second, that connection is not confined to surface issues. A look at the historical pattern of regulation shows that the movement in labor markets has followed the course of that in agricultural markets. It is important to trace out the parallels.

FREEDOM OF CONTRACT IN LABOR MARKETS — ANOTHER EASY CASE

Our initial question asks, what is the ideal regime with respect to labor contracts? The first point is to note that possible weaknesses of a consistent libertarian position on taxation, infrastructure, collective goods, and the like do not bear very strongly on labor markets. These are bilateral private arrangements that have little to do with the provision of collective goods. Twenty years ago, I wrote an article entitled "In Defense of the Contract at Will," which offered an explanation as to why employers and employees might rationally choose to adopt a form of labor contract that allowed one side to quit and the other to fire at will, for good reason, bad reason, or no reason at all (Epstein, 1984). The point is that if parties choose this arrangement, then the state ought to second-guess that choice on the ground that it ought to supply workers with some greater measure of protection, which, while beneficial to some workers once a dispute arises, is disruptive to intelligent patterns of business behavior. The acid test is whether an at-will agreement, or indeed any other kind of agreement, gives the best reflection of the joint wishes of the parties. In the overwhelming run of cases, the answer is a resounding yes.

To make this point, my 1984 paper reviewed the standard attack on contract at will: the arrangement had to be inefficient because it allowed for arbitrary and capricious behavior by management unrelated to the needs of the firm, owing to the inequality of bargaining power between the parties. The argument has an inexhaustible appeal for it has been used to justify all sorts of regulation in labor markets, including regulations relating to minimum wages, maximum hours, and employer discrimination. It has also been used to justify labor statutes such as the U.S. National Labor Relations Act. But the argument fails for one decisive reason. It is not plausible to think that just about every employee so misunderstands his interests that he enters into transactions that leave him worse off than before or that do not reflect the value of his production to the firm. Here, as in so many other areas, free entry on the other side of the market affords the most powerful and consistent defense against arbitrary market power. Of course, there is little doubt that someone could point to the exercise of the power to fire that reflects the pettiness and incompetence of management, just as some decisions to quit are borne of jealousy and ill-temper. But the task here is not to examine under a microscope the aberrant behavior of employers and employees in a few carefully selected individual cases. In a world of millions of transactions, it is always possible to fasten onto the subset of foolish and resentful decisions, which will, it must be remembered, arise under any legal regime. Rather, the task is to find out what set of institutional arrangements will, from the ex-ante perspective, produce the best set of results in the long run. Here the initial presumption that should hold in the absence of harmful subsidies or externalities is that common patterns of behavior persist because they advance the interests of *all* parties to them. Customary practices between ordinary individuals will self-correct if they are inefficient, and the pervasive use of contracts at will at every salary level and in every occupation is strong evidence of the efficiency of the arrangement relative to its next-best alternative. The one serious matter is to identify the source of those gains.

One obvious place is in the administrative costs, both public and private, of running this contractual system. These costs are low because neither side can force the other to continue with the relationship or pay some unspecified damages associated with the breach. In some instances, under a system of freedom of contract, either by custom and practice or by contract, an employer may supply severance pay upon dismissal to give the worker some protection against dislocation. But this financial payment will be calculated by some simple formula. It will not allow courts to impose huge amounts of "consequential damages" for emotional distress and economic dislocation. It involves none of the detailed exploration of the ups and downs of a relationship in the elusive effort to determine whether the dismissal was "for cause."

Another great advantage of the at-will system is that it supplies an informal method of bonding that keeps both sides in line. The employer who tries to take advantage of the employee by altering working conditions for the worse will be met by the threat to quit, because now the deal is worth less to the employee than the wage received. So long as markets are competitive, the switching costs will be relatively low, lower in fact than they are in a highly regulated world where employers have to think twice before taking on a worker whom they may be unable to fire if things do not work out. Yet on the other side, the employee who takes it easy on the job is faced with dismissal because he is no longer worth his wages. But even here, management will hesitate to dismiss for good reasons. One is the very substantial costs of recruiting and training a replacement who might or might not turn out to be better than the worker who was dismissed. The second is that unjust dismissals could induce other workers to leave while the going is good, thereby compounding the problem of recruitment and retention. (One sign of a well-managed firm is when departing workers are willing, even anxious, to help hire and train their replacements.) The pressures in any competitive market are always intense on both sides, such that the constant monitoring of each places a powerful check against the advantage-taking by the other. Over time, as a relationship emerges, the two parties may well develop some level of trust for each other, which reduces the monitoring costs and allows them to make informal adjustments to preserve their relationship, adjustments that are far more difficult to make in any regulated environment. The at-will regime, which is precarious as a matter of law, often proves quite durable in practice. But where this contract falls short— as when one party has to perform first before the other must perform at all—then some new provision can be introduced to handle the defect. Thus, a salesperson who is paid on commission cannot be fired with impunity after the account is landed but before the commission is paid. The at-will contract is a viable option, but it is not an obligation. Parties who want periodic or term contracts are free to enter into them.

A full regime of contract requires more than an intelligent law of employment contracts. The second critical piece to any common-law scheme of labor relationships must forthrightly address how competitors and unions must deal with workers under contract with other employees. The usual and correct rule is that any employee who works only under a contract at will is fair game for a rival employer who wishes to bid up his wages. The only way in which an employer can obtain insulation from that competition is to lock in a particular worker under a long-term contract, such that the effort to lure him away becomes a form of "tampering," a tort or civil wrong that goes under the name of inducement of breach (as opposed to termination) of contract. At this point, the employer with a long-term deal has a property right of sorts in the employment contract for its duration, which is protected only against those rival employers who seek to lure away an employee during term *with notice* of the contract arrangement. When that illegal inducement takes place, the current employer has, in addition to a breach-of-contract remedy against his wayward employee, the right to obtain an injunction and damages against the third party, even if he cannot obtain a decree that requires the worker to return to work. To give the famous English example from the 1850s, the worthy Lumley entered into an engagement with the famous opera singer Johanna Wagner for several engagements for the London season. The nefarious Gye came along to bid her away. The court enjoined Wagner from working for Gye, even though it could not compel her to sing for Lumley. The point of the decision was to aver that competition is fine until people enter into specific engagements, but once they do, that person is protected from rivals. All in all, this system strikes a nice balance between the need for stability in labor relations and the need for competition in labor markets.

THE DEVELOPMENT OF CARTELS IN LABOR MARKETS

There are, of course, many refinements to the basic pattern that absorb the attention of the professional lawyer. But in line with our theme on the importance of getting the easy cases right, I shall pass by those variations. The central question for our purposes is determining how robust this common-law system is in the face of relentless efforts to cartelize labor markets. These efforts did not start with the large trade unions of the last half of the nineteenth century, but they were much in evidence in the effort of independent contractors (in contrast to employees) to organize guilds under state franchises and charters that would restrict output and raise rates for their members. Often these disputes translated into efforts by the organization to stop the activities of individual members who wished to undercut standard rates. But the rise of mass-production industries demonstrated anew the proposition previously noted about agricultural markets—namely, that those markets that are amenable to competition are equally amenable to cartelization. Now that large numbers of workers are hired to perform similar jobs in the close proximity of the plant floor, the costs of organization are relatively low when set against the anticipated gain. Here again, the fundamental challenge for the labor movement is to find ways to organize its member workers while keeping out new firms seeking entry under the cartel umbrella.

Let's go through some of the steps in the process. First, there is the question of organization itself. Can the labor union find ways to spur the coordinated activities of its members in order to raise wages above the competitive levels? If so, the question then arises as to whether these kinds of activities should be regarded as contracts in restraint of trade, which expose union organizers and members to private suits for damages, public law enforcement, or both. The late-nineteenth and early-twentieth centuries saw a halting effort to apply the laws of conspiracy and combination against unions and their members. After all, what is the difference to third parties if the increase in the price of goods and services derives from employee, as opposed to employer, efforts to maintain cartels? By the mid-nineteenth century, it became tolerably clear in both England and the United States that the legislatures and courts were reluctant to carry this program to its successful conclusion (see, e.g., *Commonwealth v. Hunt*), but there are some notable exceptions. In the famous Danbury Hatters case (*Loewe v. Lawler*), a union engaged in national secondary boycotts of the products of firms that refused to be unionized was held liable in a treble-damage action under the Sherman Act, which resulted in personal judgments being levied against its individual members (*Lawler v. Loewe*).

The antitrust laws were only one possible source of counterpressure to unionization. On the private side, of equal importance in this period in the United States was the so-called yellow dog contract (anyone who works for the employer outside the union was described as a coward or a yellow dog). This contract stipulated that an employee who agreed to work for the firm had to give that firm his undivided loyalty, so that he could not at the same time be a member of the union, either openly or in secret. These labor contracts were often on an at-will basis, so why, it may be asked, would the employer seek the additional stipulation from a worker who could be fired on the spot once his dual allegiances were discovered? The answer to this question lies in the issue of coordinated worker behavior. Large groups of organized workers have the power to shut down a mine in an instant by a concerted walkout of the sort that would count as an illegal collective refusal to deal under the antitrust laws. But rather than pursue multiple and costly remedies against this group of workers, the yellow dog contract allowed the firm to bring a single action against any union for inducement of breach of contract before the collective action struck. Injunctive relief against the outsider was a powerful antidote to unionization, but it left the workers the option, if conditions got too bad, to quit the firm and join the union. The English courts were prepared to extend the tort of inducement of breach of contract to the labor situation, and the U.S. courts followed suit. In its defense of standard common-law principles, the U.S. Supreme Court, during this period, took two strong steps to preserve this common-law regime. First, at the constitutional level, it struck down, both at the federal and the state level, efforts to impose regimes of mandatory collective bargaining on firms as a limitation of freedom of contract (see *Adair v. United States* [1908]; *Coppage v. Kansas* [1915]). Second, it held that the tort of inducement of breach of contract applied to employees and unions in the same fashion that it did to opera singers and impresarios: an injunction could be obtained against a union so that it could not engage in covert organizing activities (*Hitchman Coal & Coke Co. v. Mitchell* [1917]). The impressive generalization makes perfectly good sense as a matter of general theory because in both these divergent settings the point of the legal system is to develop a set of institutions that favors and preserves competition in both capital and labor markets. These three cases, which have been commonly and fiercely denounced, should be understood as procompetitive and not as antiunion.

CARTELIZATION AND THE POLITICAL PROCESS IN THE UNITED KINGDOM

The political forces against this procompetitive trend, however, surfaced almost immediately, and manifested themselves in different ways in the United Kingdom and the United States. In the United Kingdom, the decisive movement was the passage of the Trade Disputes Act of 1906, which contained the following key provisions. First, it insulated trade unions, as opposed to their members, from liability for tort. In so doing, it suspended the usual rules of vicarious liability that hold a firm liable for the wrongs of its employees, so long as those wrongs arise out of and in the course of their employment. The effect of this provision was to immunize unions from liability even in the case of an authorized strike. Second, the act made the actions of individual persons done pursuant to an agreement or combination actionable only to the extent that they would have been actionable without such agreement or combination. The point of this somewhat obscure position was to say that the individuals could be responsible for acts of force and violence, which are wrongs when done individually. But they could not be held responsible for any collective refusal to deal or secondary boycott, for in these cases there is no underlying act of force or fraud whose consequences are magnified by collective action. The net effect of this provision was, of course, to remove the antitrust restraint on union conduct that fell short of the use of force. And finally, the act abolished in the context of labor disputes the torts of inducement of breach of contract and other torts relating to interference of trade more generally (as by force between potential trading partners). It also eliminated torts that interfered "with the right of some other person to dispose of his capital or his labor as he wills." The net effect of these provisions was to withdraw the legal infrastructure that was intended to secure long-term market competition. And just to finish matters off, the instability of markets was further increased by a generalized practice that denied legal enforcement to any labor contract. The long history of tortuous British labor relations was fostered by this legal regime, which had the continued backing of the Labor Party. The economic dislocations that this system inflicts are surely great, even if most difficult to calculate.

CARTELIZATION AND ITS IMPLICATIONS IN THE UNITED STATES

In the United States, the traditional legal order held on a bit longer, given the Supreme Court's defense of the yellow dog contract. But alongside those judicial developments, the political forces of the "progressive" era were pushing hard in the opposite direction to create labor exemptions from the complexity of contract and tort rules needed to secure competitive labor markets.

The first stage of the counterattack was found in the Clayton Act, which exempted all labor organizations from the scope of the antitrust laws on the ground that labor should not be treated as a commodity or an article of commerce. This provision paralleled the British Trade Disputes Act and left labor free to organize for its own self-protection. There is, in this context, an instructive disconnect between the stated rationale contained in the Clayton Act and its particular legislative consequence. The normal consequence of stating that something is not a commodity or article of commerce is to treat it as a *res extra commercium*, or an item that is beyond commerce. That rule would apply to sacred objects, such as gravesites and national monuments, and carries with it the consequence that they cannot be sold or mortgaged. But clearly no one in the labor movement wanted a rule that prohibited the sale of labor through ordinary employment contracts. What they wanted, and what they were able to get, was an exemption from the requirements of ordinary competition law. They also wanted, and were able to obtain, a general rule that prevented the use of injunctive relief in the course of a labor dispute, from Section 20 of the same statute. The effect of all of this was to undermine the classical legal synthesis as it applied to labor relations.

Yet this system, for all its advantages, did not allow, in and of itself, for the effective cartelization of labor markets because it offered no effective restraint on entry by other firms. Here there were a number of tactics used in manufacturing that were not available in agricultural contexts. One of these was picketing or patrolling, which is an institution devilish to regulate even under the best of circumstances. On the one hand, pickets could be regarded as individuals who supply information to the world about the practices of the employers whom they targeted and thus are protected under any regime that prizes freedom of speech, including the First Amendment to the U.S. Constitution. But by the same token, it is easy to see how speech can become hopelessly entwined with threats, or implied threats, to use force, which is unacceptable under a classical liberal order. Beefy workers standing in mass by a plant gate could use force against the entrants, and just that fear could keep people away from the gates. What makes the matter more difficult is that picketing could also be viewed as a collective effort to obtain a refusal to deal, which carries with it strong antitrust-type implications, especially when used to organize primary and secondary boycotts. But even with all these difficulties, there is no question that picketing is one part of a comprehensive strategy to reduce entry by rivals that could otherwise prosper under the higher wage umbrella set by union negotiations.

In and of itself, picketing is probably not enough to switch the balance of advantage in labor disputes, for some people could easily treat it as a sign that the picketed firm offers lower prices than those that have the union blessing. In addition, picketing may fail to achieve its stated goals, even when it resorts to illegal activities, because it is expensive to maintain and may not prove effective against rivals who may spring up at multiple sites. So here, as with the agricultural move-

ment, it is possible to add new elements to the mix. For
the most part, this was not done in the British Labour
movement, but it was done in the American one. The
first element of the game was to withdraw the prospect
of easy injunctive relief against labor unions, which was
done in part by the Clayton Act and, much more systematically, under the Norris-LaGuardia Act of 1932,
which also declared the yellow dog contract to be
against public policy. In addition, in 1935, the U.S. system adopted the National Labor Relations Act. Impor-
tantly, this act instituted a complicated administrative
law system that allowed the majority of workers in an
appropriate bargaining unit to designate a union as its
exclusive bargaining agent. It also established a set of
statutory "unfair labor practices" for employers who interfered with union affairs, discriminated against union
members, or refused to bargain with the union repre-
sentatives.

The effect of this system was to abandon the competitive labor market with rapid movements across firms.
The intellectual mindset behind both these statutes is
easily observed from their statements of public policy.
The Norris-LaGuardia Act treats as its public policy the
assumption that the "unorganized worker is commonly
helpless to exercise actual liberty of contract and to protect his freedom of labor" (29 U.S.C. §102). The National Labor Relations Act, for its part, starts on the assumption of "[t]he inequality of bargaining power
between employees who do not possess full freedom of
association or actual liberty of contract" (29 U.S.C.
§151). There is a certain irony in both these provisions

because of their ostensible acceptance of the ideal of freedom of contract, which is said to be neither "actual" nor "full" for unorganized workers. The new implicit norm for a full and fair contract is the ability to exert monopoly power and the correlative duty of the firm to bargain with workers who have opted by election for the collective bargaining solution. But the principle here is not capable of systematic generalization. The employer, in all cases, has no ability to refuse to deal, but must negotiate in good faith, without having to make any particular concessions to union demands. The system, therefore, creates a bilateral monopoly situation that is calculated to impose high transaction costs on unions and management alike. The law of good-faith bargaining has itself generated an immense amount of complex litigation as to the topics that must be addressed and the pattern of bargaining that must be followed. The firm, for example, that makes a take-it-or-leave-it offer runs the serious risk of being hit with a charge of "unfair labor practices" under the act.

It is important to understand the major inversion of legal rules that is required by the adoption of this scheme. The most obvious change is in the law of contract, for it is no longer possible for an employer to walk away from a transaction. There is now a duty to deal that makes the standard industrial firm resemble a common carrier—with, of course, obvious differences, because there is no rate schedule typical of regulated industries. But once there is a duty to deal, the traditional rules of property have to give way as well. Employees have a right to engage in organizing efforts that take advantage of the employer's property, at least to the extent that it is not done on the work floor or during working hours. The rules on speech become special as well. While the general American tradition calls for free and robust debate, labor law has its own tradition of speech in which the unilateral promise of benefits or threats amounts to unfair labor practices. These rules create immense difficulties in their application, but it would be a mistake to indicate that they have left employers utterly without resources on their own behalf, for the ceaseless debate over labor legislation before the National Labor Relations Board, and in the courts, has not allowed the union movement to run roughshod over a determined management opposition. But our concern here is not with the question of partisan advantage but with that of social loss. While it is easy to imagine worse paths that U.S. labor law could have taken, I am hard-pressed to believe that this statute could produce any net social gain at all, let alone one that exceeds the extensive administrative costs of its own implementation. When one cuts through the endless details and complexities, what we see is the statutory codification of a preference for monopoly over competition—an easy case wrongly decided.

To understand the full picture, however, it is necessary to understand the limitations as well as the influence of the National Labor Relations Act. This labor statute may create a state monopoly for the individual firm that has been organized, but it does not stop new firms from springing up in competition with them. The issue for the labor movement, therefore, has been how to block these new forms of entry. One strategy is to support various forms of legislation that make it difficult for people outside the union to underbid those in it. That decisive step does not, of course, protect the workers who are thrown out of jobs because they are not allowed to underbid their union rivals. The point here is to protect the union from competition by setting, for example, the statutory minimum wage above the competitive level that other workers could hope to earn but below that which unions could secure for their workers through collective bargaining. Maximum hour and workers' compensation require a somewhat more complex story, for here these statutes, although apparently neutral, were prepared in a fashion that had a disparate impact on the smaller nonunion firms, which had higher compliance costs than larger unionized establishments. In the United Kingdom, because Parliament was supreme, there was never a constitutional battle as to whether these statutes were consistent with either private property or freedom of contract. But in the United States, it is no accident that maximum hour and minimum wage laws were subject to important constitutional limitations under the older legal order (*Lochner v. New York* [1905]), which also looked with hostility on any system of collective bargaining. But these constitutional limitations were quickly undone under the New Deal (*West Coast Hotel v. Parrish* [1937]).

Questions of individual rights were, however, not the only issues implicated in the U.S. experience. The huge expansion of federal power under the commerce clause that I noted in connection with the agricultural

cases was preceded five years earlier by an identical
movement in labor cases. The earlier law did not allow
for the national regulation of local manufacturing or
agriculture (*United States v. E.C. Knight Co.* [1895]),
and thus made it difficult for any state to impose a strong
system of worker protection in the face of the exit threat.
Earlier efforts to impose a national child labor statute
had been rebuffed on the grounds that federal government could not assume control over local matters by
refusing to allow goods made by firms that had used
child labor in their operations (not necessarily on the
goods shipped) to be kept out of interstate commerce
(*Hammer v. Dagenhart* [1917]). Local governments did
not refuse to enact child labor statutes, but they sometimes allowed children to work at a lower age than any
proposed national statute. But with the New Deal, the
sharp change in attitude toward labor statutes carried
over to matters of federal power. The lower courts all
struck down the National Labor Relations Act as beyond
the scope of Congress, but the Supreme Court broke
with its earlier precedent and allowed the statute to take
hold (*National Labor Relations Board v. Jones & Laughlin Steel Corp.* [1937]). The attitude that it was for the
federal government to determine whether to support
competition or monopoly became the dominant motif
in both areas. In the end, the labor movement was able
to achieve its two major goals: the ability to organize its
own members and the ability to get state assistance in
the exclusion of rivals.

RESTRAINTS ON UNION POWER

The question is, what was gained by this powerful struggle? What is interesting from a comparative perspective is that the U.S. system, with all its legal requirements and administrative rigidities, probably proved more successful than the British, which withdrew legal protection from labor relations altogether. Within the British system, a determined union could exert enormous economic power without fear of disenfranchisement. Within the American system, a number of powerful factors have tended to blunt the effectiveness of unions. First, the original 1935 New Deal statute was subject to extensive revisions under the Taft-Hartley Act of 1947. That statute was passed in response to the rash of strikes and industrial unrest that followed World War II, and it tended to make the path of unionization more difficult than it had previously been. A separate set of unfair labor practices directed toward unions were introduced into the statute, including a number that limited their power to engage in secondary boycotts. A widespread set of union corruption issues provoked further regulation under the Landrum-Griffin Act of 1959. The judicial interpretation of these statutes has not been markedly promanagement or prounion, so that the initial legislative compromises have, by and large, remained stable over the past fifty years.

In addition, the secular shift toward smaller firm units, which characterizes modern economies, has complicated the task of organizing workers. Most important, perhaps, the strong, if erratic, free-trade impulse has exposed unionized firms to global competition even in such industries as steel, where the ill-considered tariffs imposed by George W. Bush in 2001 represented a most regrettable error before it was reversed at the end of 2003. The increased foreign competition in such industries as automobiles has effectively taken the strike option off the table for the major U.S. producers because unions well understand that any strike for higher wages is likely to cause a major loss of market share or bankrupt the firm on whose success their own success depends. In general, I think that globalization is the most powerful force at work here. If individual firms within an industry do not sit on a secret cache of monopoly profits, there is little that a union can achieve, no matter how skillful its leadership or aggressive its bargaining strategy. The change in public sentiment toward free trade has had a very market-positive influence on the degree of labor power.

6. Conclusion:
The Importance of Getting the Easy Cases Right

IN THE END, everything is connected with everything else. Markets survive and societies prosper because they get enough of the easy cases right by embracing competitive solutions. It would be nice to report that these carry the day in situations where they should work well. But the experiences that we have had, and continue to have, with labor and agriculture indicate how difficult it is to secure a sound social result in the face of partisan and factional pressures that work to undermine them. In place of markets, we are all too often treated to the spectacle of complex legal arrangements that provide object lessons in economic pathology and opportunities for lawyers and expert witnesses to enrich themselves by working on disputes that ought never to arise in the first place.

Within the U.S. and European cultural framework, it often proves very difficult to win the major intellectual battle on the dominance of competition, although I think it is a terrible mistake not to try. But it is possible to win some second-order decisions about the fine-tuning of these various systems, which can mitigate some of their adverse effects. It is fair to say that in terms of the agricultural situation, the technological improvements have partially offset political mistakes, at least in the developed countries. And I think that within the United States and the United Kingdom, the new waves of technology and the expansion of the international trade system have mitigated some of the power of national monopolies. But this is not to say that we have reached, or are capable of reaching, a final resting place in the struggle between open competition and state-created monopoly. The settings that make competitive markets work well are the identical settings that make cartels possible. Our future success in picking the right policy alternative is, and will remain, dependent on the ability of people to persuade themselves that one set of outcomes is better than the other. Otherwise, the political process will not support voluntary models but may, in the end, generate forces so strong as to gobble all of them up.

References

Adair v. United States, 208 U.S. 761 (1908) (federal railways).

Allnut v. Inglis, 12 East 525, 104 Eng. Rep. 206 (K.B. 1810).

Black, C. (2003). Franklin Delano Roosevelt. *Public Affairs*.

Clayton Act 38 Stat. 730 § 6 (1914), 15 U.S.C. § 17.

Commonwealth v. Hunt, 45 Mass. (4Met). 111 (1842).

Coppage v. Kansas, 236 U.S. (1915) (state laws).

DeSoto, Hernando. (2000). *The Mystery of Capital: Why Capitalism Triumphs in the West and Fails Everywhere Else*. New York: Basic Books.

DeSoto, Hernando. (1989). *The Other Path: The Invisible Revolution in the Third World*. New York: Basic Books.

Epstein, R. A. (1984). In Defense of the Contract at Will. *University of Chicago Law Review*, 51: 947.

Epstein, R. A. (1985). *Takings: Private Property and the Power of Eminent Domain*. Cambridge, MA: Harvard University Press.

Epstein, R. A. (1993). *Bargaining with the State*. Princeton, NJ: Princeton University Press.

Epstein, R. A. (2003). *Skepticism and Freedom: A Mod-*

ern Case for Classical Liberalism. Chicago: University of Chicago Press.

Hammer v. Dagenhard, 247 U.S. 251 (1917).

Hayek, F. A. (1944). *The Road to Serfdom*. Chicago: University of Chicago Press.

Hitchman Coal & Coke Co. v. Mitchell, 245 U.S. 229 (1917).

Labor Management Reporting and Disclosure Act of 1959, 73 Stat. 519, as amended, 29 U.S.C. § 410–531.

Lawler v. Loewe, 235 U.S. 222 (1915).

Lochner v. New York, 198 U.S. 45 (1905).

Loewe v. Lawler, 208 U.S. 274 (1908).

Lumley v. Gye, 2 El. & Bl. 215, 118 Eng. Rep. 749 (K.B. 1854).

National Labor Relations Act 49 Stat. 449, as amended, 29 U.S.C. 151–69.

National Labor Relations Board v. Jones & Laughlin Steel Corp., 301 U.S. 1 (1937), reversing *NLRB v. Jones & Laughlin Steel Corp.*, 83 F.2d 998 (5th Cir. 1936).

Nebbia v. New York, 294 (1934).

Norris-LaGuardia Act 47 Stat. 70 (1932), as amended, 29 U.S.C. 101-115.

Olson, M. (1965). *The Logic of Collective Action*. Cambridge, MA: Harvard University Press.

Parker v. Brown, 317 U.S. 341 (1943).

Trade Disputes Act 6 Ed. VII ch. 47.

United States v. E. C. Knight Co., 156 U.S. 1 (1985).

United States v. Wrightwood Dairy, 315 U.S. 110
    (1910).
U.S. Constitution Art I §8.
Webb-Pomerene Act 291 U.S. 502 (1934).
West Coast Hotel v. Parrish, 300 U.S. 379 (1937).
Wickard v. Filburn, 317 U.S. 111 (1942).

Commentary by
Geoffrey Wood

THIS FASCINATING ESSAY by Richard Epstein, originating, as Geoffrey Owen notes in his foreword, in the 2003 Wincott lecture, is in a field unfamiliar in Britain — that of Law and Economics. In Britain, these two disciplines are often regarded as separate. An excellent book treating law and economics as a linked and coherent subject (Veljanovski, 1990) has been out of print for more than ten years.[1] Few British universities offer even a single course on law and economics as a part of a degree, and where interest is shown, it is often solely by lawyers. Economists, by and large, neglect the discipline, despite its importance in the work of, for example, the Office of Fair Trading. It is as well, therefore, to start by offering a definition of the field before proceeding to point out some highlights in Richard Epstein's fascinating and stimulating paper and drawing from them some inferences of particular relevance to Britain, and to Europe generally, in the present day.

Geoffrey Wood is professor of economics, Cass Business School, London, and wishes to acknowledge Charles Goodhart for his most thoughtful comments on an early version of this commentary.

1. I understand that the IEA plans to publish a new book on law and economics by the same author in the near future. This will be a welcome addition to the sparse European literature on the subject.

Cento Veljanovski defined Law and Economics as follows: "The economics of law can be defined rather crudely as the application of economic theory, mostly price theory, and statistical methods to examine the formation, structure, processes, and impact of the law and legal institutions." He then went on to separate the field into "Old" and "New." "The old law and economics is concerned with laws that affect the operation of the economy and markets," he wrote, while the new "takes as its subject-matter the entire legal and regulatory systems irrespective of whether the law controls economic relationships. In recent years contract, tort (the area of the common law which deals with unintentional harms such as accidents and nuisance), family law, criminal law and legal procedure have all been subject to economic analysis" (Veljanovski, 1990, 14, 15).

These definitions are clear and helpful, but they are one-sided. They suggest that economic analysis can be used to help understand the workings and consequences of law. The subject is more wide ranging than that. Law can help us understand economic outcomes and structures. In other words, we can either start as economists and analyze the workings of the law or start with the law and show how it can affect economic outcomes.

The "new" law and economics is the field of Richard Epstein's paper. What is the subject of the paper? Epstein's central point is that it is important to get certain big and straightforward issues right. The more complex issues, which attract much attention, although not unimportant—they can sometimes involve substantial expenditures—are unimportant by comparison with a few really big issues. The basic reason for this is that the hard cases involve a great deal of effort and still have a high failure rate. We can see with hindsight that the wrong decision was made, or, on other occasions, we remain unclear that the right decision was made. An example is the decision to build a new airport. Enormous costs are involved, and there are consequences for many aspects of life—for "noise, pollution, traffic, land values, business growth, and the like," to quote Epstein. Such is the complexity of that one-off decision that it is easy to be wrong, even with the best will and ability in the world.

Before leaving these difficult one-off issues to one side, though, it is surely worth considering whether a way can be found of establishing a common framework in which to deal with such problems. By removing some of the "one-off-ness," the costs of each decision would be reduced. Surely a way of doing this that is worth exploring is to consider establishing, by law, a form of market framework; a sketch of such a one follows.

Those proposing to build a new airport (for example) and those opposed to it could be required to register sealed bids: the first of how much they would pay in compensation for building the airport, the second of how much they would pay to stop its being built. Thus could be determined how much the airport was worth to each party if built on that spot; whichever party offered more would make the payment to the other side and then have its way.[2]

2. This proposal exploits the Coase theorem (1960) on externalities,

What we do not have to live with, and most certainly should not live with, is neglect of easy cases that have important ramifications. What are these easy cases? The most important one, and the topic of Epstein's lecture, is "how a society draws the interface between market choice and government behavior. . . . The truly great social catastrophes . . . arise from a wholesale disrespect for individual liberty . . . and from a total contempt for private property." Be right on these big issues and much good will follow; be wrong, and "unnecessary social losses" are guaranteed, and catastrophe is possible.

Epstein opens his argument by considering socialism and its associated collectivism as a means of organizing production. Wholesale and complete collectivization is and always will be a failure. If the required information were available to government, it would become available to the citizens, who would try to undo the socialist attempt to separate what is produced from the distribution of that product. "As the night follows the day, every clever government intervention will invite multiple private responses, which are certain to undo whatever good might have come about if dedicated government officials (itself a generous assumption) had exclusive use of the new technologies involved."[3] It is un-

---

avoiding the usual cost problem by restricting the scheme to where large sums are involved. It was the expense of such negotiations relative to the resulting benefits that led Coase to stress that his analysis revealed how to look at the problem of externalities rather than providing a universally applicable way of dealing with them.

3. The observation about government officials may take British readers a little aback. The public choice analysis of government is both better

fortunate that Chancellors of the Exchequer, and finance ministers more generally, do not yet fully recognize this, for if they did, they would abstain from the continual tinkering with taxes, incentives, and regulations that preoccupies so many of them; but they do at least refrain from wholesale nationalization.

Next he turns to the libertarian alternative. This starts from the presumption that "voluntary transactions are presumptively preferred because they are positive-sum games from which both sides benefit." For such transactions to be common and multiply, there needs to be a framework of law to define and defend property rights, for without such rights there can be few such exchanges of titles to ownership. The markets, Epstein urges, cannot generate these laws themselves.[4] He cites DeSoto's example of street addresses, "without which it is impossible to organize a system for delivering the mail or supplying electricy, gas, police, and fire service." That a framework of law is necessary is surely correct. We should, however, be careful not to concede government too great a role. DeSoto's example is excellent to illustrate the point. London was the first city to have street numbers, following an act of Parliament of 1765. But that act followed a private initiative. The first street to

---

accepted and more widely used in the United States than in the United Kingdom. Possible reasons for this are discussed in Capie and Wood (with F. Sensenbrenner) (2004). A major part of the explanation may lie in the traditionally nonpartisan nature of the British Civil Service, at least until recently, even at the very highest level.

4. Jonathan Sacks (2002) has also argued this position, with an only partially overlapping set of analytical tools.

be numbered was Prescott Street in Whitechapel in 1708, numbered at the initiative of its residents, concerned with delivery of at least some of the services Epstein lists.[5] Nevertheless, the scope for such private initiatives is limited to small groups—the costs of negotiating soon rise as the numbers of participants do and inhibit nongovernment-organized action. We must therefore focus on how to judge and restrict laws.

Where, Epstein asks, does the "simple logic of voluntary contracting" lead us in addressing that matter? His basic proposition is that there should be no compensation for losses incurred through the operation of competitive markets.[6] This was traditionally defended by lawyers distinguishing between harm and actionable harm. An actionable harm, such as arson, destroys capital. Loss by, for example, not getting a contract because another supplier is cheaper does not destroy capital, leaves the firm that did not get the contract to transact again, and lets two parties gain from a mutually beneficial exchange. That is a brief summary of the economic argument that Epstein advances for a legal conclusion. He then applies it to two important markets:

5. DeSoto's acceptance that street numbering requires state action is reminiscent of the acceptance of many writers of economics textbooks that the state had to organize the provision of lighthouses to guide ships, because lighthouses provided a good for the use of which charging was not possible. As was discussed by Coase (1988), provision was in fact organized privately by groups of shipowners.

6. Asymmetries of information may, in some cases, produce qualification to this; but the existence of these is most plausible in financial markets, which Professor Epstein does not discuss.

that for agricultural goods and that for labor. Both these markets have been cartelized by government action, legislating with what, no doubt, appeared the best of motives but, Epstein demonstrates, to the harm of society in general.

Agriculture in the United States is supported by producer subsidies, as it was until recently in the European Union. (The changes to the EU system that are soon to take place will break all links between current production and current subsidy; farmers will be paid for having been farmers in the past.) A producer subsidy system has to be buttressed by restrictions on production and on entry. This has served to keep prices unnecessarily high and to inhibit the kind of entry that would promote consumer choice. Much of Richard Epstein's discussion of agriculture is based on evidence from the United States, but the EU's Common Agricultural Policy was at best similar (many would argue much worse) in its harmful effects domestically, and it also did international harm. It did that politically, of course, by creating grounds for international disputes, but it also contributed to poverty in underdeveloped countries—for agricultural surpluses are shipped to these countries, thus destroying the fragile prosperity of their domestic farmers. Then, in further abuse of European taxpayers, taxes are spent in an attempt to relieve the poverty caused at least in part by the agricultural policy that residents of the EU are taxed to support.

Problems arise, too, in the cartelization of labor markets, which has been produced by legislation supporting trade unions and giving them immunity from many of the legal actions that cartels of producers would face. The result has been that unionized industries have maintained higher prices and innovated less in both products and production methods and sometimes, in consequence, gone into decline that might well have been avoidable had their labor market been different. Examples, admirable for the forcefulness of the demonstrations they provide are, first, Britain's formerly nationalized industries of gas, electricity, and telephones, which have lowered prices and innovated when the joint labor cartels and producer monopolies were destroyed; and second, the British motor car industry, greatly reduced in size by competition from abroad and that had its life made easy for it by the rigid labor market of Britain's industry.

Of course, the biggest thing of all that follows from the "simple logic of voluntary contracting" is free international trade. This not only maximizes the benefits of exchange with any existing pattern of producers, but it also moves these producers toward an efficient structure; for free trade injects into every economy blessed by it a virus—the virtuous virus of competition—which destroys monopolies and cartels through the entry of new firms. If a country has free trade, then the harmful effects of protecting various groups through domestic policies are at least mitigated, and may well be eliminated altogether. Get free trade, and much else good will follow.

Should we adopt free trade unilaterally, or should we, rather, adopt it only in exchange for similar moves by other countries? It has been traditional for economists to argue that unilateral adoption is desirable. Joan Robinson put the case with brevity and clarity; she observed that if other countries have rocks in their harbors there is nevertheless no reason to throw rocks into your own. And the same applies to tariff barriers as to such physical ones.

This conclusion is correct provided there is no possibility that, by negotiation, the other countries will reduce their trade barriers. But as Epstein points out, it is necessary to consider not only the initial effect of any measure but also subsequent effects. It thus becomes worthwhile asking what the impact of trade liberalization made conditional on trade liberalization by another country will be. An early example of this being taken into account is the repeal of Britain's Corn Laws in 1846. Sir Robert Peel, the then prime minister, was persuaded of the benefits of free trade by the economists of the time. (Frank Fetter [1980] provided an account of the parliamentary part of their activities.) The Corn Laws were repealed as an act of unilateral trade liberalization. The action was unilateral because the countries of continental Europe would not negotiate to reduce their tariff barriers, and Peel eventually decided that it was in Britain's interest to liberalize alone. This led to Britain's becoming a free-trading nation.

Peel hoped that Britain's actions would lead to what Bhagwati (2002) called "sequential reciprocity," or to other countries' following Britain's lead, seeing how Britain had benefited from free trade and hoping to benefit likewise. There was subsequent trade liberalization, but, as Richard Conybeare (2002) pointed out, although the liberalization was clearly *subsequent*, it is not possible to either confirm or deny that it was *consequent*.[7]

Are there advantages to actions that lead other countries to liberalize their trade? Although a formal demonstration that there are such additional advantages is not straightforward, the intuition is clear. If both countries liberalize then each can specialize to a greater extent in producing those goods that it is comparatively better at, and consumers in *both* countries have cheaper access to goods that satisfy their tastes. Hence, although Epstein's principle that there should be no compensation for losses incurred as a result of the workings of a competitive market, and its natural extension that there should be no protection from the working of such a market, seems to suggest that free trade should be adopted regardless of foreign behavior, there is a case for multilateralism, provided that its end result is sure to be free trade.

This, it must be said, is not as easy as it may sound. Consider two countries entering into trade negotiations. One country wants both countries to achieve free trade but will adopt free trade even if the other does not; the other is perfectly content if the first country achieves free trade but does not wish to achieve that itself. If that second country knows the first will eventually abandon protection regardless of the behavior of the second, then the first has little if any bargaining power. Nevertheless, the game is worth playing. Free trade for both may be

---

7. An extensive discussion of these issues can be found in Bhagwati (2002).

the outcome—not necessarily immediately or even after the first set of negotiations, but as the protectionist country comes to see the advantages free trade brings to both consumers and producers in the free-trading country. (Producers gain as a result of, among other factors, their becoming more efficient as a result of competition and thus doing well in markets outside their home one.)

The current trade negotiations at the World Trade Organization are an example of where these issues should be thought about seriously by economists. We know that there are gains from unilateral free trade and that there are even greater gains from multilateral free trade. These are among Epstein's "easy cases." What is harder to determine is whether a multilateral or a unilateral course is the better one to pursue in any particular set of trade negotiations.

It is now convenient to move on to certain very recent actions of policy makers, every one a consequence of neglecting Epstein's basic principles of supporting freedom of contract and considering subsequent, as well as first-round, actions, which although of apparently minor significance at the present time are likely to have numerous harmful consequences in the future. These relate to the limitation of working hours in place in most of the European Union and the Trade Secretary's ruling in the case of the proposed takeover of Safeway, the British grocery chain. These are discussed in turn, before we return in conclusion to Professor Epstein's lecture.

Working hours were limited supposedly as a way of helping workers, and also, it was suggested by some, as a way of creating jobs for at least some of the large number of unemployed in parts of continental Europe.[8] This is, of course, another example of the interference with the labor market that Richard Epstein discusses. Interference with freedom of contract in this manner will impinge particularly on some types of workers and industries. Long hours worked over a period of the year, for example, are for some industries an efficient way of organizing production. The workers in these industries (and in any industry where long hours per week, although not necessarily every week, are an efficient way of working) are made less productive by this law. They will continue to be employed only if their wages fall. Thus, they suffer rather than benefit from a law designed to protect them. The working time directive and associated labor market regulations are, in Epstein's terminology, "easy cases." They break the fundamental principle of freedom of contract—and in this case have the opposite effect from that intended.

The Safeway ruling moves us to some new issues and also directs us to a section of Epstein's arguments that we have not yet mentioned. It is useful first to outline the issue. A grocery store, Wm. Morrison, made a bid for Safeway. This triggered interest from other grocery stores. It was decided that a takeover could affect competition, so a review was undertaken by the Com-

---

8. Explaining the fallacy behind the belief that by restricting working hours there will be a proportionate rise in the number of workers employed would be aside from the theme of this paper. It is discussed in Wood (2002).

petition Commission. On the basis of this review, the secretary of state decided that only Wm. Morrison could take over Safeway. This ruled out a competitive bidding process for the company, unless some bidder not in the grocery business decided to mount a takeover, and none did. Accordingly, it is highly likely that shareholders in Safeway will not do as well as they otherwise would from the takeover. Now, what are the objections to that outcome, setting aside the obvious one that shareholders in Safeway could make? What harm, except to them, has interfering in a voluntary contract done?

Suppose there had been no interference and a higher price had been paid for the company. This would have increased the incentive in similar future cases for shareholders in a firm that was doing less well than others in the market to put pressure on the management to either improve or be sold. (Imposing such pressure is not costless, in either time or money.) This increased incentive would mean that the economy's productive resources were wasted for less time, and that is to the good of everyone, not just shareholders in the company.

To this argument that there should have been no intervention, there may be opposed the claim that concentration in the grocery business would have increased as a result of such an unhampered takeover, and that such concentration would have reduced competition to an extent that could well have outweighed the benefits just described. It is somewhat contentious to claim that concentration reduces competition; it is the existence of barriers to entry that allows monopoly profits, and these barriers do not necessarily rise with the concentration of

the industry. But be that as it may, an approach to cartels mentioned by Epstein is relevant whatever one concludes on that issue. Do we need to worry about cartels,
provided that agreements between cartel members are
not enforceable at law, and especially if new firms can
enter the cartelized industry? There are arguments for
this approach; and there are arguments that lead to the
more aggressive anticartel policies of the United States
and Britain. But as Epstein points out, whatever one
concludes on this matter, the approach of considering
legal intervention to prevent cartels is completely incon-
sistent with the attitude that has been taken to the agriculture and labor markets. The Safeway case involves
a (relatively) minor issue—policy toward cartels—but it
leads us to a big one. Allowing freedom of contract in
competitive markets is of major importance; governments have recognized that principle. It is too important
to be applied only where politically convenient.

Professor Epstein's paper is a stimulating one, rich
in powerful insights that can help us not only understand the world better but actually improve the world
and make every person in it better off, or at least capable
of being so. Law and Economics is a discipline little
studied in Britain, but it provides such a powerful set of
tools that its neglect cannot be justified. I very much
hope that this absorbing lecture encourages not only the
use in Britain of the kinds of ideas set out in it but also
the study and teaching of the subject, so that there are
many practitioners engaged in public policy formation
and analysis in this country. This could not but improve
both the laws that constrain private actions and public

policy and the conduct of policy within the set of laws that constrain it.

REFERENCES

Bhagwati, Jagdish (ed.). *Going Alone: The Case for Relaxed Reciprocity in Freeing Trade*. Cambridge: MIT Press, 2002.

Capie, F. H., and Wood, G. E., with F. Sensenbrenner. "The Political Economy of Foreign Investment in the UK," in H. Huizinga and L. Jonung (eds.), *The Internationalisation of Asset Ownership in Europe*.

Coase, R. H. The Problem of Social Cost, *Journal of Law and Economics*, 3(1): 1–44.

Coase, R. H. The Role of the Lighthouse in Economics, in *The Firm, the Market, and the Law*. Chicago: University of Chicago Press, 1988.

Coneybeare, John. Leadership by Example?: Britain and the Free Trade Movement of the Nineteenth Century, in J. Bhagwati, *Going Alone: The Case for Relaxed Reciprocity in Freeing Trade*. Cambridge: MIT Press, 2002.

Fetter, Frank Whitson. *The Economist in Parliament 1780–1860*. Durham, NC: Duke University Press, 1980.

Sacks, Jonathan. Markets, Governments and Virtues, in F. H. Capie and G. E. Wood, *Policy Makers on Policy*. London: Routledge, 2002.

Veljanovski, Cento G. *The Economics of Law: An Introductory Text*, Hobart Paper (Institute of Economic Affairs, London.)

Index

Adair v. United States, 59
Adam, 4
agriculture, 28–43; cartelization of, 36–37, 43; Clayton Act and, 37–38; Congress regulation of, 40; as easy case, 35–42; in European Union, 83; government dispensation to, 24–26, 27, 28–30, 31; insulation of, 33–34, 35; intellectual property and, 48; political sympathy for, 31; production increase for, 33–34; right to farm in, xix–xx, 33–35; state intervention in, 28, 33–34; state-protected/organized, xxv–xxvi, 36–37, 38–39; subsidies for, xx, 35–36, 45–48, 83; tariffs/protectionism in, 45–48, 49; technological advances in, 71–72
Allnut v. Inglis, 44–45
American legal education, 1–2
antitrust laws, 25–26; as counterpressure to unions, 58; exemption from, xx; U.K., unions and, 62
Arnold, Benedict, xiv
at-will agreement: administrative costs of, 53; dismissal, cause and, 53–54; informal method of bonding and, 54; labor and, 51–56, 58; rival employer and, 55–56; self-correcting, 53

bargaining, 52; collective, 55–56, 58, 59; exclusive agent, 55; good-faith, 65
Bhagwati, Jagdish, 85
bill of rights, second, 34
Black, Conrad, 8
Blackstone, 3
boycott, secondary, 60–61, 63. *See also* picketing
Brandeis, Louis, xxv
Bush, George W., xiv, 70
buyer, willing, 35

Caplan, Bryan, xvii; *The Myth of the Rational Voter: Why Democracies Choose Bad Policies*, ix–x
cartels/cartelization: of agriculture, 36–37, 43; antitrust laws and, 25–26; cheating amongst, 26, 27, 28, 38; classical liberal and, 39; competition and, 25–32, 39, 84; destruction of wealth by, 27; development of, in labor, xxvi, 56–60; harm from, 26, 66; judiciary resistance to state-sponsored, 42, 44, 58–59; labor market, 51–70, 83–84; minimalist strategy and internal failure of, 26–27; monopoly and, 22, 25, 26; new members, pricing and, 33; preconditions

cartels/cartelization (*continued*)
for, 25–32; private, state blocking
of, 27; prohibition against, 32;
self-interested, 42;
standardization of products for,
24–25; state-protected/sponsored,
xxv, 38–39, 44, 46, 72; tariffs
and, 40; in United Kingdom,
60–61, 71; in U.S., 61–68
cases, easy, 4, 7, 71–72; agriculture
as, 35–42; classical liberalism
and, 10, 19, 21–22, 26, 31, 63;
freedom of contracts in labor
markets as, 51–56, 88;
multilateral free trade as, 86, 87;
between socialism/libertarianism,
9–13, 17, 18, 20
cases, hard, 4, 5–6, 23, 79; between
socialism and libertarianism, 9–
13
Chancellors of the Exchequer
(U.K.), 68
cheating, cartels and, 26, 27, 28,
38. *See also* corruption; fraud
Chiang Kai-shek, 8
child labor, 68
choice: public, x–xi, 80n3; "yes or
no," 6
classical liberalism. *See* liberalism,
classical
Clayton Act, 37–38, 51, 62, 64
Coase theorem, 79n2–80n2, 82n5
coercion: state, vii, ix, 13–14, 17–
19; taxation, finance and, 17–19
collective bargaining, 55–56, 58, 59
collectivism, 10–11, 12, 68
command-and-control economy,
xxiii
commerce, beyond, 62
commerce power: affirmative, 42–
43; of Congress, 40–42, 58;
dormant/negative, 41–42
Commonwealth v. Hunt, 58

compensation: competitive harm,
19–23, 28, 82; worker, 67
competition, 61; cartels and, 25–
32, 84; exemption from, with
state-cartel, 39; foreign, 70; free
trade with, 71, 73; labor and
exemption from, 61, 62;
precondition for, 25–32; pricing
and, 30; rival employer, contracts
and, 55–56; state monopoly, new
firms and, 66–67; state power
enforcing, against collusive
agreements, 28; Supreme Court
rulings on, xx
Competition Commission (U.K.),
89
competitive harms, competitive
markets/compensation for, 19–
23, 28, 82
competitive markets: competitive
harm compensation and, 19–23,
28, 82; freedom of contract
allowed in, 90; means of
production organized by, 9, 88;
standardization of products for,
28–29
concentration, industry, 89–90
Congress: agriculture/
manufacturing regulation by, 40;
commerce power of, 40–42, 58
constitution, U.S. written, 3
constitutional doctrine: intellectual
attack on, xxvi; mistakes in, xxiv
contracts, 38, 82; breach of, 53,
55–56, 59, 61; employer forced
to deal with, 56–57; free,
limitations on, xxvi; freedom of,
51–56, 59, 88, 90; long-term,
55–56; yellow dog, 58–59. *See
also* at-will agreement
Conybeare, Richard, 85–86
Coppage v. Kansas, 59
Corn Laws (U.K.), 85

corruption, in labor, 60. *See also* fraud

criticism, standard of, 7

currency, tariffs and reducing demands on, 49

deflation, 36

democracy, 50. *See also* liberal democracy

DeSoto, Hernando, 17, 69n5, 81–82, 82n5

developing countries, Western subsidies damaging, xx, 83

difference in errors, 6–7

dismissal, 53–54

distribution, ix, 11–12, 31; ignorance, xi–xii

dormant commerce clause, 41–42

easy cases. *See* cases, easy

economic fatalism, 9

economics, law and, 76–78

economy: command-and-control, xxiii; decentralized, 16–17; integrated national, 37; private law governing unregulated, 1–2

employer, rival, 55–56

English legal education, 1–2, 77

English private law, 1–2, 22, 44–45

Epstein, Richard, 10

errors, 5, 6–7

European Union, 83

Eve, 4

evil, source of, 4

farm. *See* agriculture

fatalism, economic, 9

favoritism, political, 16

federal power, expansion of, 44, 67, 68

federalism, 3

feedback mechanism, x–xi

Fetter, Frank, 85

Financial Times, 3

flat taxation, xi

fraud, 13–14, 20, 60–61

free contract, limitations on, xxvi

free speech, 63

free trade, 47–48, 49, 69, 84–87; multilateral, 86, 87; tariffs and, xv, xvi; unilateral, 49, 84–85

freedom of contracts, 51–56, 59, 88, 90

gain: competitive markets/trade, 22; mutual, xx, 15, 19; specialization, 36

Germany, 8

globalization, 70

goods/services, 11–12, 17, 22, 25, 34; overproduction of, from subsidies, 46

government: agriculture dispensation by, 24–26, 27, 28–30, 31; agriculture without intervention of, 28; behavior, 6; competition policy against collusive agreements by, 24; against excessive individualism, xxv; federal power expansion and, 44, 67, 68; labor dispensation by, 24–26, 27; limited, classical liberalism and, xii, 16; price regulation by, 45–46; private markets needing, 16; public choice analysis of, 80n3; separation of power in, xxiv; takeover's regulation by, 88–89; voluntary exchange regulation by, 16, 84, 89. *See also* commerce power; judiciary; state-sponsored cartels resisted by

grocery business, 89

Grotius, 3

guilds, 57

H-1B visas, xvi

Hale, Matthew, 44

Hammer v. Dagenhart, 68
hard cases. *See* cases, hard
harm (loss): actionable, 21, 82; with actionable injury, 21, 69–70; from cartels, 26, 66; compensation for, 19–23, 28, 82; competitive, 19–23, 28, 82; without injury, 21, 69–70
Hayek, Friedrich, 8, 11
Hitchman Coal & Coke Co. v. Mitchell, 59
Hitler, Adolf, 8
human character, 14

ideas, great, 3
ignorance, xi–xii, xiv, xvii
immigration, xvi–xvii
immunity, official, 7
income/wealth, 11, 13; cartel's destruction of, 27
independent contractors, 57
individual, 24–25; deception of, 14
individual liberty, 7–8, 80
individualism, excessive, xxv
industry, concentration of, 89–90
infrastructure projects, 17–18
injunctive relief, 59, 62, 64
intellectual attack, on constitutional doctrine, xxvi
intellectual property, 5–6; agriculture and, 48
interest groups, market rigged by, xix

judiciary, state-sponsored cartels resisted by, 42, 44, 58–59

Kennedy, John F., 15
Kerry, John, xiv

labor: antitrust law exemption of, xx; antitrust laws as counterpressure to, 58; at-will contract with, 51–56, 58; bargaining of, 52, 55–56, 58; cartel development in, xxvi, 56–60; Clayton Act and, 37–38, 51, 62, 64; corruption in, 60; dismissals, recruitment and, 53–54; exemption from competition with, 61, 62; freedom of contracts in, 51–56, 88; governmental dispensation to, 24–26, 27; organization of, 57, 59, 62, 64, 68, 69–70; picketing by, 62–63; political sympathy for, 26; restraints on, 69–70; self-protection by, 62
labor market, cartels in, 51–70, 83–84
laissez-faire, 1
Landrum-Griffin Act, 69
law: antitrust, xx, 25–26, 58, 62; Corn, 85; economics and, 76–78; private, English, 1–2; tort, 56, 59, 60, 61, 78
Lawler v. Loewe, 58
lawsuits, individual, 22–23
legal education, 1–2, 77
liberal democracy, 9; challenge of, 17; coercion systems, taxation and, 17–19
liberalism, classical, 1–8; cartels and, 39; easy cases and, 10, 19, 21–22, 26, 31, 63; inversion of, 37, 39; limited government approach of, xii, 16
liberalization, trade (U.K.), 85–86
libertarianism, 13–19; antitrust law not part of, 25–26; competitive markets, competitive harms' compensation and, 19–23; easy cases between socialism and, 9–13, 17, 18, 20; hard cases between socialism and, 9–13; self-interest assumed by, 14, 15; social infrastructure underplayed by, xxi; strengths of, 13–15;

voluntary exchange, social gains and, xxi, 13–15, 68–69; weakness of, 16–18

liberty, disrespect of individual, 7–8, 80

Lochner v. New York, 67

Locke, John, 3

Loewe v. Lawler, 58

losses, social. *See* harm

manufacturing, Congress regulation of, 40

Mao Tse-tung, 7

market: arbitrary, power, 52–53; choice, 6; failures of, 12; inferior structure of, with cartels, 27; public systems needing private, 16; special problems in, 12–13; state intervention in, 12

means of production: collectivism weakness for, 10–11, 12; competitive free markets organizing, 9, 88

medical ethics, 17

mercantile transactions, 20

mercantilism, 48

minimum wage, xii–xiii; immigration and, xvi–xvii

monopoly, 21; bilateral, 65; cartel, 22, 25, 26; fear of, xxv; new firms/competition and, 66–67; price regulation, government and, 45–46; rate of return limited for, 45; rival, 31; state, for decentralized economy, 16–17; state-protected, xxv–xxvi, 44, 46, 72; technology mitigating, 71–72. *See also* cartels/cartelization

Morrison, Wm., 88–89

multilateralism, 86, 87

mutual gain, xxi, 15, 19

The Myth of the Rational Voter:

Why Democracies Choose Bad Policies (Caplan), ix–x

National Labor Relations Act, xx, 52, 64–65, 68; limitations/influence of, 66–67

National Labor Relations Board v. Jones & Laughlin Steel Corp., 68

national socialism, socialism v., 8

nationalization, 12–13

natural reason, 3

natural resources, 4

Nebbia v. New York, 46

neutral groups, political support, 30

New Deal, xxv, 38, 67, 69

Nixon, Richard, xiii

Norris-LaGuardia Act, 64

Office of Fair Trading (U.K.), 77

outsourcing, xiv

parity principle, 33–34

Parker v. Brown, 38–39

Parliament, 58

patents, 4–6

Peel, Robert, 85

Peru, xv

picketing, 62–63

planning, excessive, 12

political favoritism, xxi

political rhetoric, xi, xiii

political sympathy, for agriculture, 31

positive-sum games, 14

predation, 27

price controls, xiii–xiv

pricing: cartels and, 26–27, 33; competitive, 30; determination of, 37; discrimination of, 30; fixed, 34; government regulation of, 45–46; lower, for maximizing profits, 50; maintenance of, 34; monopoly and, 45–46; as

pricing (*continued*)
  restraint of trade, 35–38;
  stabilization, 41
private cartels, state-sponsored, 38–39
private initiatives, 81–82
private law, English, 1–2
private property, 13, 68; contempt
  for, 7–8, 80; limitations on, xxvi;
  security for, 16
private welfare, social and, 23
production, agricultural increase
  for, 33–34
products: fungible, 28;
  individualized, 24–25; raw, 50;
  standardization of, 28–29
progressive era, 61
progressive taxation, ix
Progressives, xxv
property rights, 7–8, 13, 14, 16, 68,
  80; intellectual, 5–6, 48
prosperity, social, 9
protectionism, vii, 35, 41, 42, 73;
  subsidies, tariffs and, xvi, 45–48,
  49
public choice theory, x–xi, 80n3
public goods, rules for provision of,
  xxi
public interest, 46
Pufendorf, 3
pure transfer games, 14

rate of return, 45
Reagan, Ronald, xii
reciprocity, sequential, 85
recruitment, costs of, 54
res extra commercium, 62
restraint: labor, 69–70; trade, 27,
  35–38, 48, 57
Ricardo, David, 49
right to farm, xix–xx, 33–35
The Road to Serfdom (Hayek), 8
Robinson, Joan, 85
Roman legal education, 1–2

Roosevelt, Franklin D., xix–xx, 34,
  38; misguided economic policies
  of, 8

Sacks, Jonathan, 81n4
Safeway, 88–89, 90
self-correction, 53
self-help, 16
self-interest, 14, 15, 42
self-protection, 62
sequential reciprocity, 85
Sherman Act, 37, 38, 50
Skepticism and Freedom (Epstein),
  10
Smith, Adam, xxv, 26, 48
Smoot-Hawley tariff, 42
social improvement, 20
social welfare, private and, 23
socialism: computer calculation
  debate for, 9–10; easy cases
  between libertarianism and, 9–
  13, 17, 18, 20; hard cases
  between libertarianism and, 9–
  13; national socialism v., 8;
  weakness of, 9–11, 68
socialist calculation debate, 11
Soviet Union, 8
specialization gain, 36
Stalin, Joseph, 8
standard of criticism, 7
standardization, of products, 28–29
state: agriculture dispensation from,
  24–26, 27, 28–30, 31; coercion
  by, vii, ix, 13–14, 17–19;
  monopoly for decentralized
  economy, 16–17; private cartels
  blocked by, 27; -protected/
  sponsored cartels, xxv, 38–39, 44,
  46, 72. *See also* Congress;
  government
state intervention: in agriculture,
  28, 33–34; in market, 12, 24–26
street address, 17, 81–82
strike, 60, 69, 70; in U.K., 52

subsidies, xx; agricultural, xx, 35–36, 45–48, 83; overproduction of goods from, 46; public benefit for, 46; tariffs, protection and, xvi, 45–48, 49
supermarkets, 31n1
supply and demand, 21, 34
Supreme Court: competition rulings by, xx; dormance commerce clause and, 41; National Labor Relations Act supported by, 68; yellow dog contract defended by, 59

Taft-Hartley Act (1947), xx, 69
takeover, 88–89
tariffs, xiv, 34, 42; agriculture, protectionism and, 45–48; cartels and, 40; currency, reducing demands on, and, 49; free trade and, xv, xvi; reducing, 85; steel, xiv–xv, 70; subsidies, protection and, xvi, 45–48, 49
taxation, viii–ix, xi; flat, xi; liberal democracy, coercion and, 17–19; progressive, ix
technology, 71–72
term contracts, 55–56
territorial principle, 50
tort law, 56, 59, 60, 61, 78
trade: liberalization of (U.K.), 85–86; negotiations, 85; restraint of, 27, 35–38, 48, 57. *See also* free trade
Trade Disputes Act (U.K.), 60, 62
trade unions. *See* labor

unions. *See* labor
United Kingdom (U.K.), 52, 62, 68; cartelization in, 60–61, 71; Competition Commission in, 89;

law, economics and, 65–66, 76–77; Parliament as supreme in, 58; takeover regulation in, 88–89; trade liberalization in, 85–86
United States (U.S.), cartelization in, 61–68. *See also* Supreme Court
United States Department of Agriculture (USDA), 43
United States v. E.C. Knight Co., 68
U.S. v. Wrightwood, 43
USDA. *See* United States Department of Agriculture

Veljanovski, Cento, 77, 78
visas, H-1B, xvi
voluntary exchange, 13–15; free trade from, 84; government regulation and, 16, 84, 89; libertarianism, xxi, 13–15, 68–69; security for, government regulation and, 16; undue influences on, 20

wage, minimum, 52, 67
Wagner, Johanna, 56
wealth. *See* income/wealth
The Wealth of Nations (Smith), 26, 48
Webb-Pomerine Act, 39
welfare, social/private, 23
West Coast Hotel v. Parrish, 67
Wickard v. Filburn, 44
Wincott, Harold, xix, xxi, 4, 9
worker: compensation, 67; protection, 68; unorganized, 64
working hours, 87–88
World Trade Organization, 42, 47, 48, 87

yellow dog contract, 58–59